BENJAMIN BRITTEN

BENJAMIN BRITTEN

Alan Kendall
Introduction by Yehudi Menuhin

Macmillan

© Macmillan London Limited 1973

All rights reserved. No part of this publication
may be reproduced or transmitted, in any form or
by any means, without permission.

SBN 333 15226 3

Designed by Paul Watkins and Florianne Henfield

First published 1973 by
Macmillan London Limited
London and Basingstoke
Associated companies in New York, Toronto,
Dublin, Melbourne, Johannesburg and Madras

Phototypeset by Richard Clay (The Chaucer Press), Ltd,
Bungay, Suffolk
Printed by BAS Printers Limited,
Wallop, Hampshire

Contents

1 Road to success / 8

2 The return to England / 22

3 Conductor and Festival Director / 44

4 Composing for the voice / 59

5 Art of the composer / 70

6 Britten's philosophy / 84

7 Conclusion / 97

Catalogue of Works / 106

Index / 111

Bibliography / 112

Acknowledgements / 112

To the boys and staff of St George's School, Windsor Castle

Author's acknowledgements

I should like to thank Benjamin Britten, together with the editor of the Aldeburgh Festival Programme and Messrs Faber & Faber, for his great kindness in allowing me to quote from his speeches and programme notes, and to Peter Pears for the passage from his *Armenian Holiday*, as well as for reading the manuscript and for his valuable comments. The opinions expressed are, however, those of the author.

Thanks are also due to Peter Clamp, for first drawing my attention to the Purcell passage on English music; my old friend Georgina Powley for her patience and enthusiasm; Miss Rosamund Strode; Peter Tranchell; Patrick Wilkinson and David Willcocks.

The following kindly gave permission to quote copyright material: The BBC for Edward Greenfield's article on *Owen Wingrave* in Radio Times; Messrs Faber & Faber (*Tribute to Benjamin Britten on his Fiftieth Birthday* and W. H. Auden's *Anthem for St Cecilia's Day*); David Higham Associates Ltd (*British Composers in Interview*); The Estate of Harold Owen and Messrs Chatto & Windus (Wilfred Owen's *The Parable of the Old Men and the Young*); Oxford University Press (the composer's note to the score of *Simple Symphony* and *Henry Purcell, 1659–1695*); and Tempo Magazine (article by Benjamin Britten).

Introduction

What is an introduction? Is it in this case a preliminary canter through the familiar landscape of a character whom one both loves and admires, in which one tries as best one can to share the joys of the scenery with the reader; or should it be something more static: a worthy pronouncement of the qualities and accomplishments of the subject of the ensuing book?

Given the limitations of my own literary skills and the unique nature of Benjamin Britten, my choice must be the former, not the latter style, not the least because the occasion which prompts this book, that of his sixtieth birthday, seems so improbable, so unrepresentative in terms of actual age versus spiritual age, that to express myself in rigid fact would in no way bring to life my picture of Ben – an evocation rather than a portrait. What springs immediately to the mind's eye is how quite amazingly, how completely Benjamin Britten represents his people – their particular genius and their contemporary evolution. His imagination, formed by the sea and the elements of wind and water, with all in fact that is Nature and the countryside, at one with the literary, the poetical and those myriad subtleties which are the glory of England, her people and her land. And so is he at one with the hearts of his countrymen in their concern for their fellowmen and their sense of responsibility to future generations.

This is his greatness, his uniqueness. As he listens to the sea, so does he listen and give form to the as yet unspoken and unsung, to the yearnings and feelings even to the unborn thoughts of his people – of *all* his people, from the fishermen to the poets. A lone and supremely sensitive sounding-board, he does not pronounce or indulge himself in the manner of the romantic, nor of the didactic neither buccaneer, schoolmaster, nor academic, but reserves himself for that which he chooses to allow to play upon him. Thenceforward he communicates in terms of music to us, his audience, what he hears while listening – be it to Schubert, to a storm, to poetry, and the experience is distilled through his Englishness, his deepest self conveying a truth and a trust that carry complete conviction. His ear, inner and outer, is of such a keenness that it never fails to note the special and so different qualities of sound, of colour, of temperament of those interpreters for whom he composes, adding thereby an extra sureness of touch to all his works.

Benjamin Britten at three-score years has retained a youthfulness, a perennial innocence and that idealistic passion that is so rare. Perhaps that is the secret of his wonderful feeling for and understanding of children, to which some of his most touching and profound works testify.

How fortunate he is and how well-deserved is his country's tribute!

The whole-hearted gratitude of the British people will bring him the comfort and satisfaction which are the due of one who, deeply rooted in his own background, has all his life listened with sympathy, with compassion and understanding to all those sounds which in their turn have composed him and his civilisation, from the still small voice to the roar of the multitude, from the seas to the song of the nightingale, from the poet to the street-crier, and who has transmuted them to us all in such beautiful and moving works.

Yehudi Menuhin, 22nd November 1973

Chapter One
ROAD TO SUCCESS

BIRTH

BRITTEN.—On November 22nd, at 21, Kirkley Cliff, Lowestoft, to Mr. and Mrs. R. V. Britten—a son.

Opposite: The South Pier in Lowestoft, Britten's birthplace, photographed in the year of his birth. The composer's mother was secretary of the town's flourishing choral society, and it was she who gave her son his first piano lessons. From the outset the sea, so vital to Britten's inspiration, was thus present in his conscious

Below: Jan van Eyck's portrayal of St Cecilia, the patron saint of music, from the Mystic Lamb altarpiece in the cathedral of St Bavon, Ghent. Britten's birthday falls on the saint's day, and in writing his *Hymn to St Cecilia* to W. H. Auden's text, Britten revived an old tradition going back to Purcell, one of his favourite composers, and beyond

Blessèd Cecilia, appear in visions
To all musicians, appear and inspire;
Translated Daughter, come down and startle
Composing mortals with immortal fire.

So runs the refrain in Auden's words for Britten's *Hymn to St Cecilia*, and it was a happy coincidence that the composer should be born on St Cecilia's day (22 November) in 1913, since she is the patron saint of music.

Edward Benjamin Britten was the youngest of four children (two boys and two girls), and the family lived at Lowestoft, where the father was a dental surgeon, and the mother was honorary secretary of the local choral society. It was doubtless through his mother that Benjamin Britten's interest in music was first aroused. She had, by all accounts, a pleasant soprano voice, and a fairly catholic taste in music. Moreover, in her capacity as secretary of the choral society, visiting professional musicians engaged to sing in Lowestoft would be invited to the house, and the young Britten had a chance to meet them. Mrs Britten gave her son his first piano lessons. When he was eight he went to a local piano teacher, Ethel Astle, and at ten he started having harmony lessons. He had already started learning to play the viola by this time.

Britten's father did not want a radio or gramophone in the house because he feared it would deter the family from making music for themselves. This is a belief that his son still holds, and in spite of the benefits of radio, the gramophone, and nowadays the tape-recorder, he regrets the facility with which people may have music at their finger tips today. Another legacy from father to son was his taste for Dickens, and Britten tries to read one of his books each year.

It was through Britten's viola teacher that Britten took his next step towards being a composer. Audrey Alston was a friend of Frank Bridge (1879–1941), and when he came to Norwich in 1927, Britten was taken to meet him. Britten had been present in 1924 when Bridge conducted a performance of his suite *The Sea*, and although he was so young, he was very impressed by the music. Bridge was also, incidentally, a first-class viola player. From then on Britten used to go and see Bridge regularly in holidays from his prep school and public school, either in London or Eastbourne, and the rigorousness of Bridge's approach was something that has stood Britten in good stead all his life. Bridge would send the young Britten to

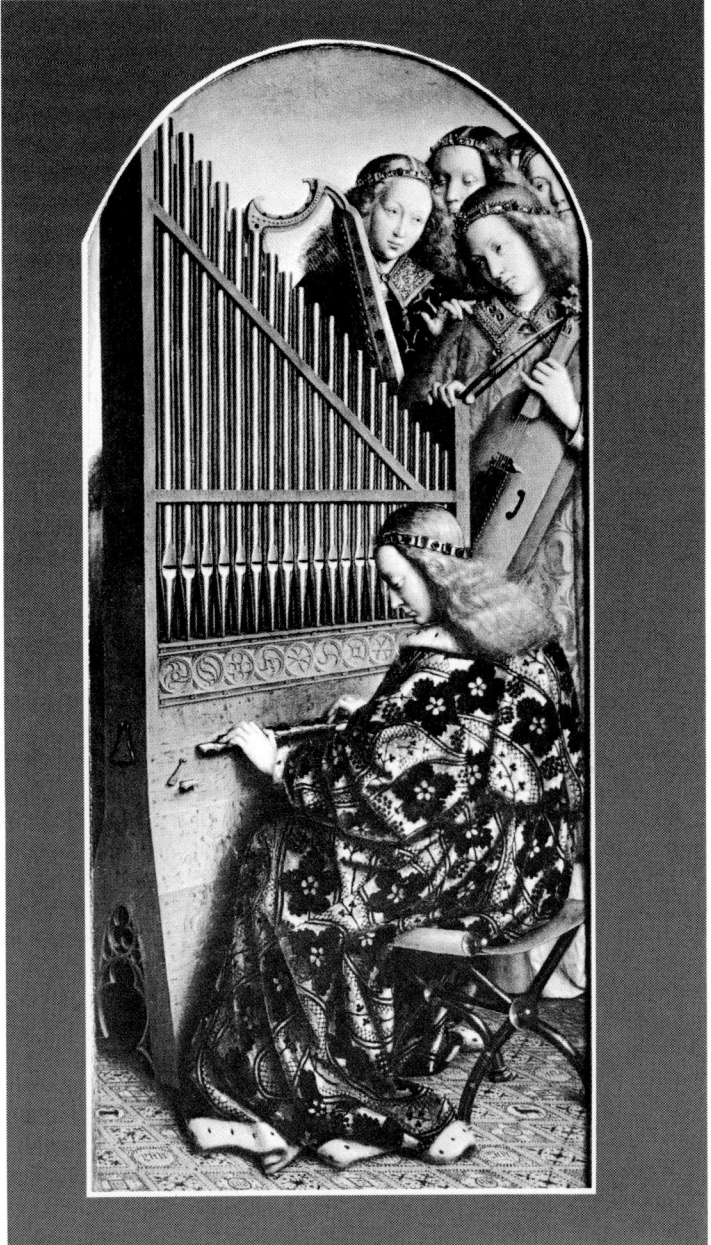

Britten met Frank Bridge, his first composition teacher, at the Norwich Triennial Festival in 1927. He had been present three years earlier, however, when Bridge conducted his suite *The Sea* at the centenary festival. An extract from the programme note then might almost refer to Britten's music that was to come: 'Objective rather than subjective in character, it never sacrifices clarity of design to realism . . .'

A concern for high technical and professional standards was one of the gifts that Bridge handed on to and developed in the young Britten. Bridge was meticulous about his score marking, and so is Britten. Even a simple thing such as the opening plainsong hymn from Britten's *The Prodigal Son*, seen here, has precise indications as to the composer's intentions for dynamics

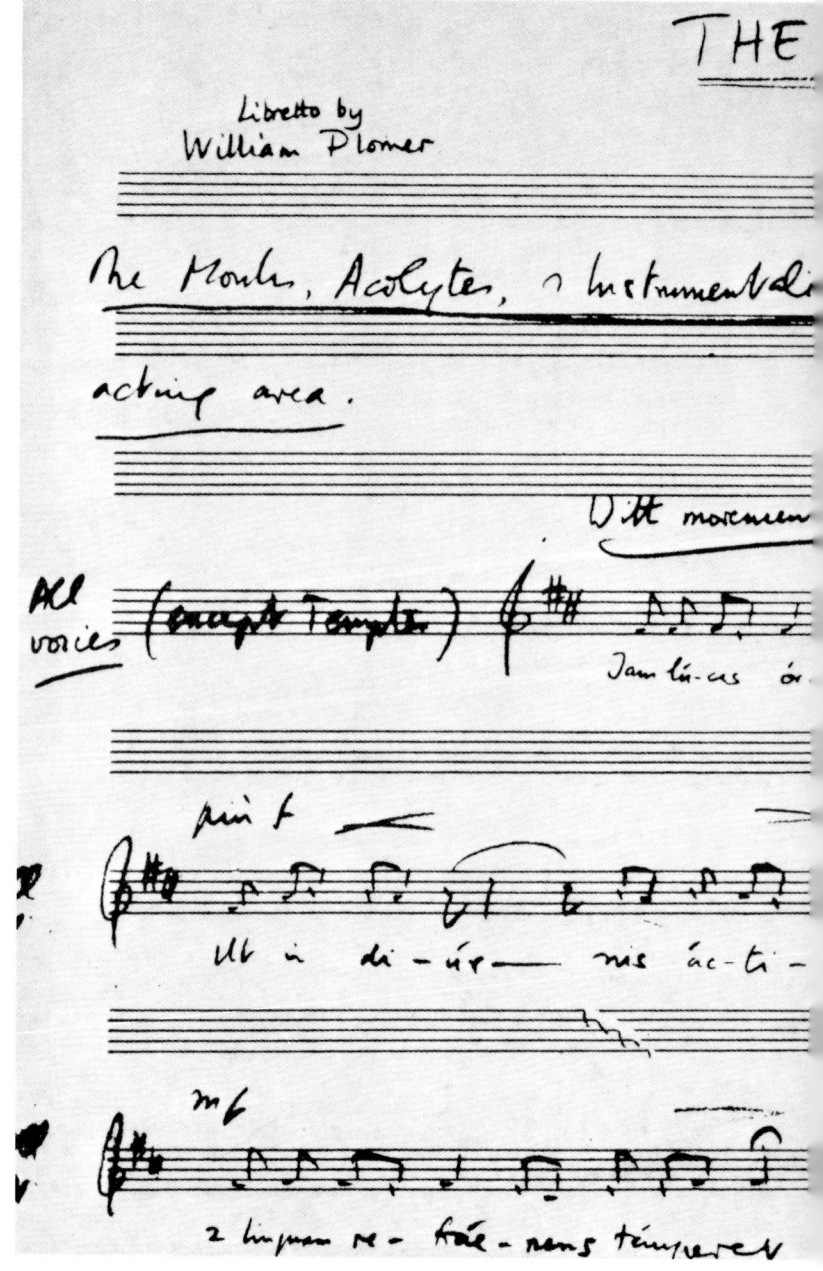

the other side of the room and then play what the boy had written, on the piano, and ask him if that was what he had intended to write. In fact by then Britten was already an extremely conscientious composer, even before he started going to Frank Bridge, and he marked every detail on his scores for his performers. This is still true, and when performers take the trouble to study their scores they find ample directions. Occasionally the lesser-known Italian musical terms that he used in the earlier music baffled them. In more recent music he has stopped using these terms so that there could be no possible doubt of his intentions.

From his prep school Britten went to Gresham's School, Holt, in Norfolk. The music master there was alarmed that one of his pupils should like Stravinsky, and the other boys were surprised when they found Britten reading scores in bed, but this was offset by the fact that there was so much more music-making going on around Britten than there had been before. In any case, he continued going to Bridge during the holidays, and had piano lessons from Harold Samuel in London. In addition to this increased musical activity, the general atmosphere of the school was, for those days, fairly enlightened. This, in conjunction with Bridge's pacifism, formed Britten's own ideas at an early stage. Bridge did not browbeat Britten into copying his own ideas, however, but he made him think and argue. Writing a tribute to Bridge, Britten said: 'In everything he did for me, there were perhaps above all two cardinal principles. One was that you should try to find yourself and be true to what you found. The other – obviously connected with it – was his scrupulous attention to good technique, the business of saying clearly what was in one's mind. He gave me a sense of technical ambition.' Britten has never forgotten his teachers from those early years, and what he owed to his family. Several of his works are dedicated to them by way of gratitude. The *Sinfonietta* (Op. 1) is dedicated to Frank Bridge, as well as *Variations on a Theme of Frank Bridge* (Op. 10), and Aldeburgh festivals help to perpetuate Bridge's music by including his works from time to time in their programmes.

Britten next won an open scholarship in composition to the Royal College of Music, London, and went there in the autumn of 1930. He studied piano with Arthur Benjamin, and Bridge suggested that he should go to John Ireland for lessons in composition. Ireland said that Britten worked very hard, and

Below: The Mercury Theatre, in London, provided Britten with the first opportunity for his works to be heard in public, at the Macnaghten-Lemare concerts organised there. His unpublished *Phantasy* for string quintet, in one movement, was first heard there in December 1932

Bottom: Alban Berg (1885–1935) has always been one of Britten's favourite composers, and it was his intention to go and study with him in Vienna at the end of his last year as a student, on a small travelling scholarship he had been awarded. His parents were advised against this by the Royal College of Music, however, on the grounds that Berg would not be a good influence

that when he first arrived at the college, Ireland knew that Britten had one of the finest musical brains the college had seen for many years. But Britten has said that he feels he did not learn very much there, and that not enough account was taken of the really gifted musician. Ireland said that when he tried to get a scholarship for Britten, one of the adjudicators said: 'What is an English public school boy doing writing music of this kind.'

Only one of Britten's compositions was ever performed at the college whilst he was a student there – the *Sinfonietta* for ten instruments – and even then after it had first been performed elsewhere. When he wrote a request for Schoenberg's *Pierrot Lunaire* in the college library suggestions book, it was turned down. When he was given a small scholarship for study and travel abroad in his last year he hoped to go to Vienna to have lessons with Berg, but his parents were advised that it would not be a good thing. The implication was that there was something slightly immoral about Berg, certainly about his music, but he remains one of Britten's favourite composers to this day.

At the age of nineteen Britten determined to earn his living as a composer when he left the college in 1933. Through the Macnaghten-Lemare concerts that were given in the Mercury Theatre in Notting Hill Gate in London, his music began to be heard by the public for the first time. It was here, for example, in 1933 that his two part-songs for mixed chorus and piano were heard. The words of the first are by George Wither, and the second by Robert Graves, an early indication of how wide-ranging Britten's choice of texts was to be. Nevertheless Britten had to earn a living. At this time John Grierson had assembled a group of very gifted people at the GPO Film Unit, and in 1935 Britten was taken into the fold. He had written the title music for a GPO film in 1933, and four others soon followed before he was asked to write the music for *Coal Face* and *Night Mail*, which are two of the finest documentaries in the history of cinema and which were to be very significant in view of Britten's future. In July 1935, Basil Wright the director took Britten down to Malvern to meet W. H. Auden who was teaching in a preparatory school there, since Britten and Auden were to work together on these two films. So began the association that was to be highly formative for Britten at this period of his life. Also, on 25 November of that same year, Britten signed a contract with the music publisher Ralph

Louis NacNeice, born in 1907, a member of the Auden and Isherwood circle who influenced Britten in his decision to go to America. Britten wrote music for MacNeice's translation of Aeschylus' *Agamemnon* in 1936, his play *Out of the Picture* in 1937, and their last collaboration was on a radio play, *The Dark Tower*, in 1946

Hawkes, to whom *Our Hunting Fathers* was dedicated. He was to stay with the firm of Boosey and Hawkes for almost thirty years.

With a group of friends – in particular Louis MacNeice and Christopher Isherwood – Auden was looking for ways and means of propagating his political ideas. He was against fascism in its several forms, and it was not surprising, therefore, that Britten, with his pacifist outlook, and he should see eye to eye on certain matters, and that their collaboration should eventually extend beyond the immediate context of the GPO Film Unit.

Possibly *Our Hunting Fathers* (1936) was the most notorious of their collaborations – Britten thinks that it was the most successful – whilst it was Auden who introduced Britten to the works of John Donne and Rimbaud, and thereby provided him with two of his most fruitful sources of inspiration. *The Holy Sonnets of John Donne* for voice and piano were written in 1945, and *Les Illuminations*, for high voice and string orchestra, in 1939.

The conditions under which Britten had to work at this time were good training. He usually had to work at great speed for the film unit, sometimes in very unfavourable circumstances, and often at times when he did not particularly feel like writing music. It was no doubt through this that the University Orator was able to say, when Cambridge University made Britten an honorary Doctor of Music in 1969, 'He likes composing works on commission – a rare quality...'

Most creative artists would probably agree that they would prefer to give expression to their artistic vision as and when they felt moved, rather than be obliged to produce a work of art to order. Naturally commissions stimulate artists, whilst at the same time providing them with a livelihood, and of course there are those who would rather work at their art, on commissions, than not at all. Britten goes much further than this, and in Chapter Six it will be seen how it is a part of his philosophy not only to accept commissions willingly, but to make music much more closely bound up with the sort of occasions that produce commissions. In other words, far from the artist being isolated in an ivory tower dedicated solely to his art, Britten wants to see him as an integral part of the community. This is why he likes composing to commission, because in so doing he is directly serving his fellow men. The conditions imposed by any one commission do not therefore become restrictions for him,

W. H. Auden and Christopher Isherwood collaborated on three plays for which Britten wrote incidental music. They are seen here about to set off for China in 1938 to report on the Sino-Japanese war. The following year they were to go to America when it seemed that there was no longer any future for them in Europe

but a challenge. His early work writing music for films gave him invaluable experience in this respect.

There was a very limited budget for these documentary films in any case, so even less was available for the musical side of them. There was no orchestra, simply a group of instruments, and Britten soon became very skilled at envisaging the sort of effect that could reproduce musically, and in the simplest possible way, a wide variety of realistic sounds. *Coal Face*, for example, which is a survey of the coal industry in Great Britain, uses only piano, percussion and speaking chorus. *Night Mail* has probably become more famous as far as Britten's talents are concerned, for in it he had the task of producing the sound of a train going through a tunnel. His solution was to record the effect of a cymbal being hit, and then reverse the sound track, so that the vibrations began faintly and slowly and gradually worked up to a climax. In this instance Britten anticipated the techniques of *Musique concrète* by some ten or fifteen years.

One can see at this early stage several aspects of Britten's musical character already in the making. His ability to produce work to a given deadline; his readiness to write for unusual combinations of musical forces if necessary, and perhaps more important for his subsequent development as a composer, his ability to get behind an idea and translate it into musical language in a way that is often startlingly new, even if in retrospect it appears obvious. It is an ability to detect inner possibilities that is akin to Gerard Manley Hopkins' 'inscape,' which will be looked at in more detail in the final chapter. Britten seems to have a flair for detecting the inscape of a given musical situation, instrumental or vocal – or both.

The early experience of working with the restricted resources of the GPO Film Unit developed in Britten a concern for clarity in orchestral texture and great skill in handling it. After 1933 he went on to write an average of four scores a year between 1935 and 1939. He provided all the music himself, except for *Men of the Alps* (1936), where in addition to his own music, Britten collaborated with Walter Leigh in arranging some of Rossini's music, and then in two of the 1938 scores he collaborated with John Foulds and Victor Yates. 1937 saw his first feature film, *Love from a Stranger*. His departure to America in 1939 put an end to this sort of work, and in fact he was to write no more film music until 1946, when he produced his *Young Person's Guide to the Orchestra* (Op. 34), though this is hardly film music in the strict sense of the term. It has now firmly established itself in the repertoire not only as an introduction, with narration, to the instruments of the orchestra, but also as a piece of music in its own right. It is also symbolic that, in his concern to 're-habilitate' Purcell, Britten should have chosen a piece of music by Purcell – the hornpipe tune from *Abdelazer* – as his theme.

Alongside this work in films should be seen Britten's incidental music for stage and radio. In 1935 he wrote incidental music for *Timon of Athens*, and the following year for Louis MacNeice's translation of Aeschylus' *Agamemnon*. Both these productions were at the Westminster Theatre in London. There were two plays in 1937, *The Ascent of F6* by Auden and Isherwood, and *Out of the Picture* by MacNeice. Another Auden and Isherwood play came in 1938, *On the Frontier*, and in the same year Britten wrote the music to four cabaret songs by Auden for Hedli Anderson, and for a radio feature *Hadrian's Wall*, with script by Auden. The collaboration with Auden had begun in 1936 with the symphonic cycle for soprano and orchestra *Our Hunting Fathers* (Op. 8), and was followed in 1937 with *On this Island* (Op. 11), five songs dedicated to Isherwood, for high voice and piano, and a setting of *Fish in the Unruffled Lakes*, again for high voice and piano. Britten continued to set Auden's texts in America. There were two songs for a monologue for Dame May Whitty, and the operetta *Paul Bunyan*, and then the *Hymn to St Cecilia* (Op. 27) for unaccompanied five-part chorus, which was written on the slow voyage back to England, and is inscribed: 'At sea ... 2 April 1942.'

As far as radio was concerned, Britten had first written for the BBC in 1937, with the incidental music for *The Company of Heaven*, and then the following year for a Whitsun programme entitled *The World of the Spirit*, and the radio adaptation of T. H. White's *The Sword in the Stone*, his famous book about King Arthur. Britten's American visit also interrupted this side of his work, apart from the incidental music to a CBS broadcast of *The Rocking-Horse Winner*, but he returned to it in 1943 to write the music for Edward Sackville-West's play *The Rescue*, and for a radio feature entitled *Poet's Christmas*. Two of the items from this broadcast for unaccompanied chorus to texts by Auden have been published: *A Shepherd's Carol* and *Chorale*. In 1946 Britten wrote music for Louis MacNeice's radio play *The Dark Tower*, and the author was so

Britten conducting a rehearsal at the Aldeburgh Festival. Like several composers, Britten became a conductor largely for performances of his own music, but has since embarked on works by other composers of special significance for him

very pleased with the result that he regarded it as having added another dimension and a new perspective to his play.

Britten's growing reputation was confirmed when he was asked to write an overture to mark the opening of the BBC's Third Programme in September 1946. This is the *Occasional Overture in C*, which was given opus number 38, but with which the composer was dissatisfied and subsequently withdrew. Apart from the music for a radio feature *Men of Goodwill* for Christmas 1947, it was also the end of Britten's collaboration in radio. Since the success of *Peter Grimes* and *The Rape of Lucretia* he was now turning to the exciting world of opera, and taking his place as an operatic composer in his own right. He also withdrew from writing stage music at this time, too. In 1946 he wrote for Ronald Duncan's translation of Cocteau's *The Eagle has Two Heads*, in London, and a production of *The Duchess of Malfi* in New York. But apart from Ronald Duncan's *Stratton*, produced in Brighton in 1949, and André Roussin's *Am Stram Gram* in London in 1954, Britten was to devote himself entirely to his own creative vision.

When Britten arrived in America he was, in his own words, 'muddled, fed-up and looking for work, longing to be used.' Over and above this immediate crisis, however, was his convinced pacifism and consequent alarm at the rise of Fascism and Nazism in Europe. In 1937 he had composed a *Pacifist March* with words by Ronald Duncan, a unison song for the Peace Pledge Union, which had been founded by the Rev. Dick Sheppard in 1934. Britten and Duncan had not collaborated before, and the war interrupted any further work together, but as well as the stage works already mentioned, in 1945 Britten wrote the incidental music to a masque and antimasque by Duncan entitled *This Way to the Tomb*. The next year Duncan was asked to prepare the libretto for *The Rape of Lucretia*. He also supplied the text for the wedding anthem *Amo Ergo Sum*, in 1949.

The *Pacifist March* shows where Britten's thoughts were directed at this time. In 1938 he wrote the music for a documentary film entitled *Advance Democracy* (1939), and a song from this, to words by Randall Swingler, was published for unaccompanied double chorus, taking the name of the film. Another sign of the times as far as Britten was concerned was the next work he wrote, *Ballad of Heroes* (Op. 14), for a festival of 'Music for the People.' Written in honour of the men of the British Battalion of the International Brigade who had been killed in Spain, the text was again by Randall Swingler in collaboration with Auden. Along with the incidental music for J. B. Priestley's play *Johnson over Jordan*, this was the last music Britten composed before he left for America.

Auden and Isherwood had already gone to America early in 1939, and Auden decided to take out American citizenship. He believed that by going to America, where he had no roots, he would be able to develop freely as an artist, and Britten initially thought the same. Britten was accompanied to America by the tenor Peter Pears, who had sung with the BBC singers for two years and had been to America on two previous occasions. They went first to Canada, however. Two of Britten's works date from this period, the *Violin Concerto in D minor* (Op. 15), and *Canadian Carnival* (*Kermesse canadienne*) Op. 19. In August 1939 the first performance in America of *Variations on a Theme of Frank Bridge* was given in New York, and Britten and Pears went to hear it. Pears had some friends living at Amityville on Long Island, and they were invited to stay there, which they did for the next two years or so, making one or two visits away from time to time. It was here that *Les Illuminations* (Op. 18) was completed, and the *Seven Sonnets of Michelangelo* (Op. 22). Several works for piano were written in America, as well as the *String Quartet* No. 1 in D (Op. 25), but these will be looked at in closer detail in Chapter Five. The other important work from this period is the *Sinfonia da Requiem* (Op. 20), which is dedicated to the memory of Britten's parents.

Britten had been asked by the British Council in 1940 to write a symphony for a celebration in connection with an unspecified foreign dynasty. Britten agreed to undertake the commission provided that it did not involve him in any expression of patriotic sentiments that he did not and could not share. It then transpired that the country was Japan, and that the celebration was the 2,600th anniversary of the founding of the dynasty by Jimmu Tenno. Other European composers had also been commissioned.

The idea of a Requiem Symphony came to Britten, and he named the three movements *Lacrymosa*, *Dies irae* and *Requiem aeternam*. The scheme was submitted and approved. In view of the war in Europe and the fighting between China and Japan, it seemed a most appropriate theme. However, some six months after the completion of the score a bitter rejection came from the Japanese authorities, with the complaint that the Christian dogma implicit in the work was an insult to the

Britten on the beach at Aldeburgh. The call of the Suffolk coast reached him in distant America when he found a book of Crabbe's poems and read an article by E. M. Forster, and determined to return home

Below: Peter Pears and Benjamin Britten in Maine, U.S.A., in 1940 with the conductor Eugene Goossens. It was in America that Britten realised how much he was attached to his native Suffolk, and determined to return to it as soon as possible

Bottom: Britten at Glyndebourne during the preparations for *The Rape of Lucretia*. With him is the producer Eric Crozier and the designer John Piper. Britten was at this time 34, and engaged on his third opera

Mikado. The attack on Pearl Harbour put an end to further communications and the first performance of the work, conducted by John Barbirolli, was given in New York in March 1941.

Already, however, Britten had had a long mental struggle during the previous year, which was reflected in a serious infection. When war finally broke out at the end of 1939 he had begun to wonder whether he might not, after all, have been of some use in England as a non-combatant. During 1940 he continued to ponder, and his mental struggle increased in pitch. As he began to recover from his illness in 1941, he decided that he would leave America and return to England.

The composer owed a lot to America. He had been made to feel at home there; he had been asked to write music, and his works had been performed. For his future development, however, possibly the best thing that America did for Britten was to show him where he belonged. He had gone to America deliberately, feeling that he did not belong anywhere in particular, and that in America, therefore, he could develop at will – much as

Auden had felt, in fact. MacNeice quoted Auden in a letter in *Horizon* (July 1940) as saying that 'an artist ought either to live where he has live roots or where he has no roots at all ... in England today the artist feels essentially lonely, twisted in dying roots, always in opposition to a group'. Yet Britten was to discover in the very place to which he had chosen to exile himself that he did, after all, belong somewhere, and have some live roots, and that somewhere was the very corner of England near which he had been born and to which, in 1937, he had returned to live. The way in which it happened was rather strange. Quite by chance he came across a second-hand copy of George Crabbe's poems in a Los Angeles bookshop in the summer of 1941, and at the same time he read an article by E. M. Forster in the BBC's *The Listener* about Crabbe and Suffolk. Britten now wanted to get back to England as soon as possible, but he had to wait for almost six months before he and Peter Pears could get a passage on a Swedish boat.

Then another thing happened in America that was also crucial to Britten's future, and in relation to his development as the composer was possibly even more important. Whilst he was waiting for his passage back to England he went to Boston to hear a performance of the *Sinfonia da Requiem* under Serge Koussevitzky, and afterwards Koussevitzky asked Britten why he had not written an opera. Britten had by this time read Crabbe's poem *The Borough*, and already ideas about *Peter Grimes*, as the work was to become, were forming in his mind. But an opera demands a freedom from financial pressures that young composers rarely enjoy, and Britten told him this. A few weeks later Koussevitzky announced that the Koussevitzky Music Foundation had allocated $1000 for an opera, which was to be dedicated to Koussevitzky's wife Natalie, who had died not long since.

The idea for an opera had not, of course, come completely out of the blue. Aaron Copland, writing in a volume published to celebrate Britten's fiftieth birthday, told of a visit he made to Snape in the summer of 1938, when he happened to have with him the proofs of his school opera *The Second Hurricane*. He liked to think that Britten's interest in opera for schools, and indeed the decision to go to America in the first place, resulted partly from this visit. Be that as it may, when Britten returned from America the stage was set for a completely new phase in his career. This time it was to establish him as one of the most important composers in British music.

Left: Britten photographed in October 1949 with the novelist E. M. Forster, who wrote the libretto for his opera *Billy Budd* and was a devoted friend

Below: Serge Koussevitzky, who encouraged Britten to write *Peter Grimes*, the opera that set the seal on his reputation as one of Britain's most important composers

Chapter Two
THE RETURN TO ENGLAND

A picture taken during the filming of *Peter Grimes* for television in 1969. It was the sea that called Britten back to Suffolk, the same sea that he had heard as a child at Lowestoft, and it was the ever-present sea which played so large a part in *Peter Grimes* and so helped establish him as an operatic composer of the first order

Michael Tippett, whose friendship with Britten dates from the war years, photographed at the time of the first performance of his oratorio *A Child of Our Time*, which Britten was largely responsible for organising in London, at the Adelphi Theatre, in 1944

WHEN Britten and Pears returned to England they decided to go before a tribunal for conscientious objectors. As a result they were exempt active military service and allowed to give recitals for CEMA (the Council for the Encouragement of Music and the Arts), from which the present Arts Council sprang. In September 1942 Pears and Britten performed the *Seven Sonnets of Michelangelo* at the Wigmore Hall in London, and just over a year later in the same hall Pears was soloist in the first performance of another work, the *Serenade*, with Dennis Brain playing the horn part.

During Britten's absence in America Frank Bridge had died, but he now made the acquaintance of another composer, nearer his own age, Michael Tippett. Tippett was also a conscientious objector, and at that time was musical director of Morley College in London. The college was about to perform one of Purcell's verse anthems, *My Beloved Spake*, and Walter Bergmann suggested Peter Pears' name for the tenor soloist. Britten came along with Pears to the rehearsal, and as a result of that meeting and the subsequent friendship that formed, it was for the two of them that Tippett wrote his cantata *Boyhood's End*. Britten and Pears gave its first performance at Morley College in June 1943.

Only two weeks later Tippett was in prison at Wormwood Scrubs. He, too, had been exempt military service as a conscientious objector, but had violated the terms of his exemption. He was therefore sentenced to three months in prison. By a curious coincidence Pears and Britten came to give a recital in the same prison, and Tippett was able to convince the prison authorities that his presence was needed on the platform, to turn the pages. Britten was at that time naturally very interested in Tippett's work, and he helped a great deal to secure the first performance of Tippett's *A Child of Our Time* in London in 1944.

In addition to his recitals with Peter Pears, Britten later made a tour of concentration camps in Germany with Yehudi Menuhin in the summer of 1945, after the first performance of *Peter Grimes* in the June of that year. Britten had been vaccinated for the visit, and as a result suffered a violent reaction and was in bed with a fever. It was at this time, on his return, that he wrote the *Holy Sonnets of John Donne* in the space of a week, though he had planned them before he went to Germany. The sight of so much suffering and the constant shadow of death, married to Donne's words and Britten's own mental

Yehudi Menuhin and Benjamin Britten photographed in July 1945, when the two artistes made a tour of German concentration camps giving violin-and-piano recitals. Although Britten had planned to set the Donne poems before he left for Germany, there is no doubt that the sight of so much horror and suffering acted as a spur to the composition of *The Holy Sonnets of John Donne* on his return

state, provide an extraordinary concentration of emotion that is manifest in the work itself. For a lighter side to this episode, during the tour, Peter Pears recalls, through some official mistake Britten was constantly designated as: 'Mr Button, Mr Menuhin's secretary.'

Britten was ready to start the composition of *Peter Grimes* in January 1944. He and Peter Pears had worked on the job of blocking out sections of the opera whilst in America, but Britten needed a librettist. He had considered Christopher Isherwood, but when he got back to England he realised that he would have to have someone on the spot, with whom he could communicate frequently and easily. His choice fell then on Montagu Slater.

In 1937 Britten had set a poem by Slater, *Mother Comfort*, along with one by Auden, *Underneath the Abject Willow*, as a group of two ballads for two voices and piano. Then in 1938 Britten wrote the incidental music for two one-act plays by Slater, *The Seven Ages of Man* and *Old Spain*, which were presented at the Mercury Theatre as puppet plays. *Ballad of Heroes*, written in the spring of 1939, is dedicated to Montagu and Enid Slater. Although the war had temporarily separated them, Britten had by no means forgotten Slater, and he asked him to prepare the libretto for *Peter Grimes*.

Today, when London is once again one of the great operatic capitals of the world – indeed one of the artistic centres of the world – it is perhaps difficult to appreciate fully the nature of what Britten was undertaking when he embarked upon *Peter Grimes*. Italian opera had been a constant part of the musical scene in London since early in the 18th century, but English opera had never really had a chance to blossom. This in itself was a deep psychological disincentive to any British composer. There had of course been the comic operas of Gilbert and Sullivan; *The Yeomen of the Guard* almost verges on the brink of being a serious opera, and indeed Sullivan did write one serious opera, *Ivanhoe*. Even so, this was far from heralding the actual establishment of a national operatic tradition. Stanford, Ethel Smyth, Holst and Vaughan Williams had made a start with operas in English, and the Sadler's Wells opera company (born out of the Old Vic Theatre) had works by these composers in its repertoire before World War II.

The onset of war, however, put an end to all entertainment almost overnight, though subsequently, when the Phoney War dragged on and the bombs failed at first to appear, various

Peter Pears in the role he created as the central character, Peter Grimes, in the opera of the same name. The first performance was in London at Sadler's Wells in 1945, and the opera was adapted for television in 1969, when this photograph was taken

Eric Crozier and the composer in front of the Moot Hall at Aldeburgh in 1949, the year in which *The Little Sweep* was first performed. Eric Crozier wrote the text as part of a larger entertainment called *Let's Make an Opera*. It was important as being the first major stage work by Britten almost exclusively for children

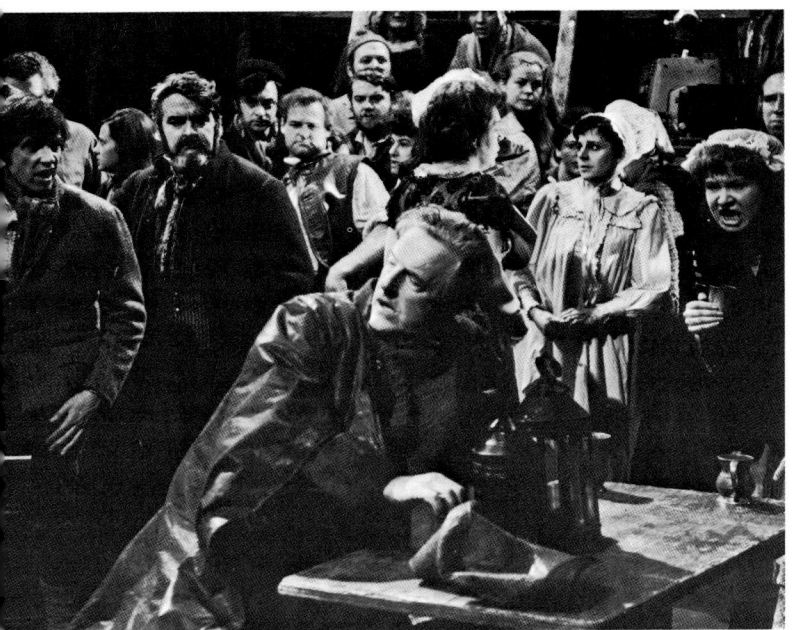

experiments, such as matinees, were tried out. Later, Covent Garden Theatre became a dance hall, and the Sadler's Wells Theatre an evacuee rest centre. The Sadler's Wells company was almost disbanded, but was able to survive at first by touring the provinces with a company that numbered twenty-five in its entirety, and then it made its headquarters at the New Theatre in London, with Joan Cross as director.

Pears was singing leading roles with the company at this time, and thanks to the support and enthusiasm of Joan Cross it was decided that Britten's opera *Peter Grimes* should be given its première by the company, and moreover that it should be the first opera given by Sadler's Wells to celebrate their return home after the war. On 7 June 1945 the theatre reopened with *Peter Grimes*. Peter Pears sang the title role and Joan Cross was Ellen. Reginald Goodall conducted – an interesting choice in view of his subsequent emergence as an esteemed Wagnerian conductor – Eric Crozier produced, and Kenneth Green designed the scenery and costumes.

With the benefit of hindsight it is possible to see how Britten led up to the writing of *Peter Grimes* in much of his previous work. He had also made one attempt at an opera whilst in America, namely *Paul Bunyan*, in collaboration with W. H. Auden. The critics were very hard on it, but the public seemed to have enjoyed it. At all events it has never been published, and during its short time on the stage was altered several times, so that it would be well nigh impossible to produce anything that could be called a definitive version. Nevertheless it was all experience for Britten.

Paul Bunyan was a legendary hero who helped pioneer the American advance into the West. He was a lumberjack reputed to be the height of forty-two axe handles, and does not, therefore, appear on stage. Only his voice is heard. The play begins before he is born, when America is still a virgin country, and ends with a Christmas party where Bunyan takes leave of his men because he has accomplished what had to be done and is consequently no longer needed. The main action of the play is concerned with the intermediate process of conquering nature. In the course of this, however, there is a conflict of personalities between the hero and two of his men. One of them is very strong but no thinker, whilst the other is thoughtful and intelligent, and therefore tends to despise brute strength.

In view of Britten's subsequent operas, there are three points

Opposite left: Benjamin Britten, Ronald Duncan and Peter Pears off for a game of tennis. Duncan provided the libretto for Britten's second opera to be staged in England, at Glyndebourne in 1946, *The Rape of Lucretia*

Opposite right: Reginald Goodall, the conductor, Britten and Rudolf Bing at Glyndebourne for *The Rape of Lucretia*. Goodall had conducted the first production of *Peter Grimes*, and alternated with Ernest Ansermet on *Lucretia*

Opposite below: Peter Pears as the central character in *Albert Herring*, in the original production of 1947. Although written for the same forces as *The Rape of Lucretia*, it was a very different work in many ways

of interest in *Paul Bunyan*. First of all, certain aspects of the construction of *Paul Bunyan*, although dictated by necessity, may well have influenced the construction of *The Rape of Lucretia*. Then *Paul Bunyan* has an almost entirely male cast, which was to be the case in *Billy Budd*, and also in *Billy Budd*, the action is not seen through Billy himself, but Captain Vere. In *Paul Bunyan* it is the thinker, Johnny Inkslinger.

Paul Bunyan was an American folk hero. Peter Grimes is in a way an anti-hero. He is a victim of society because he does not conform, yet in attempting to conform he is destroyed. The chorus, therefore, as representing society, plays a large part in this opera, not simply to comment on the action or to thicken up the vocal texture, but to act out its role in the unfolding of the tragedy. The march to Grimes' hut, where the people of The Borough hound the unfortunate man, is one of the most spine-chilling things in opera.

The use of the orchestra, too, as an element in its own right is most effective, and the interludes on the lines of tone poems give organic unity to the opera, as well as creating atmosphere and setting the scene. The texture of the orchestration vividly evokes the all-pervading presence of the sea with all its various moods and its effect on the lives of the people of The Borough.

The opera tells the story of Peter Grimes, who buys boys from the workhouse to be apprentices in his fishing business. The opera begins with the inquest on the death of Peter's first apprentice. We learn that Peter has a friend in the widowed schoolmistress Ellen Orford, and when Peter gets a new apprentice, she is going to help. The people of the Borough are apprehensive. Grimes, however, is determined to prove his worth, by making his fortune and marrying Ellen. In leaving his hut with the boy to go to his boat, Grimes is in fact embarking on his own downfall. The boy slips down the cliff and is killed, and neither Grimes, the boy nor the boat is seen for three days. The Borough suspects murder, and when Peter finally reappears, almost out of his mind, he is advised to put out to sea and scuttle the boat, rather than face the hostile townspeople.

Peter Grimes was soon acclaimed all over the world, but within less than a year it was withdrawn from the repertoire at Sadler's Wells, and those who believed in the company as a force for progress in British opera resigned. Britten did not feel that his aims were in harmony with those of the management of Sadler's Wells. A new company was formed, to be known as the Glyndebourne English Opera Company. Britten was to write a new opera for the summer season of 1946 at Glyndebourne, and it would be then taken on a tour of the provinces and to London. This then explains the limited forces required for Britten's next opera – only eight singers and twelve musicians – but that alone was not responsible for *The Rape of Lucretia* puzzling the public. The whole concept of the work was about as different from *Peter Grimes* as it possibly could be.

Britten had just written some music for a play by Ronald Duncan, so he asked Duncan to write the libretto for *Lucretia*, the idea for which had been suggested by Eric Crozier. In fact it is an adaptation of André Obey's play *Le Viol de Lucrèce* (1931). The opera tells how the Roman general Tarquin (of Etruscan origin) becomes obsessed by the virtue and chastity of Lucretia, wife of Collatinus, and goes at night to visit her. When he reaches the house he is offered hospitality, but during the night he goes to Lucretia's room and rapes her. The next morning she wakes and decides to commit suicide, but not before relating the matter to her husband.

Ernest Ansermet and Reginald Goodall were the conductors, and John Piper the designer, for the first performances at Glyndebourne in July 1946. There were several reasons for the surprised reception of *Lucretia*. After the realism of the world of The Borough in *Peter Grimes*, *Lucretia* had an unexpected formal structure with male and female chorus, in a highly stylised function. It represented a complete change of approach. Possibly the oddest thing for the audience to accept was the Christian commentary, presented by the chorus, on what was essentially a pagan theme, so that the Passion of Our Lord and the Immaculate Conception are seen against the story of Lucretia's rape and suicide. There was also a considerable amount of purely technical use of musical motif and theme, though some of the effects may well have been lost on the first audiences, and are still not perceived by any but a trained ear.

If *Lucretia* seemed a strange successor to *Peter Grimes*, then the next opera, *Albert Herring*, must have seemed even stranger for that reason. The 1946 Glyndebourne programme had announced a production of Purcell's *Dido and Aeneas* for 1947, but in fact this did not materialise until 1951. In the meantime, however, Britten and his friends decided that the Glyndebourne arrangement was not allowing them to fulfil their aims as they might wish, so the company was refounded under the name of

the English Opera Group – the name it has borne ever since, though Covent Garden is now responsible for the overall administration. It was decided that the group would, however, appear at Glyndebourne the next summer as originally intended.

This time the new opera was to have as librettist Eric Crozier, who had produced *Peter Grimes* and *Lucretia*, and the plot was taken from a short story by Guy de Maupassant, *Le Rosier de Madame Husson* (1888). The local lady of the manor – in the opera Lady Billows – wishes to choose a May Queen, but since there is no suitable candidate she decides on a May King, Albert Herring, who works in his mother's greengrocer's shop and has a reputation for being chaste and innocent. In the course of the May Day celebrations he is given lemonade laced with rum, and that evening he breaks out of his all-embracing home environment. When his absence is discovered the next morning it is feared that he is dead, and a threnody is sung. He returns, however, rather dirty and dishevelled, but pleased with the turn things took. It is in this detail that Britten's opera differs most from the Maupassant original, for there the hero really does experience debauchery, whereas Albert simply goes on a pub crawl.

The whole atmosphere of *Albert Herring*, however, is far removed from Maupassant's world. For one thing, instead of giving it a French setting, the whole opera was transported to East Anglia, and John Piper provided a suitable setting. This in itself was contrast enough with the Rome of *Lucretia*, but after rape and suicide, *Albert Herring* is essentially a comedy. Moreover the colloquial speech gave Britten great scope for following the natural inflections of the voice, which makes the recitative seem more accomplished than that of *Lucretia*. Of course Britten had had more experience by now, which is also evident in the orchestral writing. The instruments have more soloistic treatment than in *Lucretia*, and at the same time the instrumental textures that Britten achieves in *Albert Herring* are clearly much more sophisticated, particularly in view of the fact that the choice of instruments is the same. The handling of the thematic material is also more skilful, and the way in which the material is adapted, modified, metamorphosed even, is more subtle. There are several things that one might single out, but in particular – for a signpost to Britten's future development – one need only consider the children's ball game in the opera. Britten's introduction of the tune at this point, indeed his conception of it at all, was the sort of thing he was to do on several occasions later in his career. Sometimes he has used established tunes, sometimes he has written his own, but the way in which he adapts them or introduces them at given points in his works has become one of his hallmarks.

The promised *Dido and Aeneas* still failed to appear, but Britten produced instead his realisation of Gay's *The Beggar's Opera* in 1948. This was in fact the first year of the Aldeburgh Festival, which will be looked at in the next chapter, though the first performance of *The Beggar's Opera* was given at the Arts Theatre in Cambridge. It was typical that Britten should have reacted against the then existing versions of the opera, which had tended to submerge the true natures of the various airs included in it, so as to make them blend into an overall sweetness and prettiness. He wanted to restore to the airs their individual, and sometimes very subtle, melodic and rhythmic aspects. His treatment was varied and interesting, and the accompaniments were full of insights into the tunes, which they emphasised, or elaborated upon. Perhaps more significant however, for the appreciation of his individual character as a composer, was Britten's handling of the key sequences in the opera. He had always been concerned with the relationship of keys to one another, but in *The Beggar's Opera* this is developed at some length.

The second year of the Aldeburgh Festival was 1949, and Britten produced a new work for it. It was an opera called *The Little Sweep*, from a larger entertainment called *Let's Make an Opera*. In the first half of the work a group of children help three adults to devise and put on an opera, and the second half is the work itself. Here Britten was writing an opera in which ordinary children who wanted to sing and act could do so in truly professional terms. With another of Britten's imaginative strokes, the audience are given four songs to sing, so that they too become part of the action.

Audience participation nowadays, particularly in the live theatre, is a commonplace thing, but when Britten wrote the opera he was making a daring departure, which might have failed. The experience of audience participation in *Saint Nicolas* the year before, however, must have given him encouragement and inspiration.

The second half of the work, *The Little Sweep*, deals with a topic dear to Britten's heart, namely the exploitation of innocence, in the shape of a young chimney sweep. Through the

The Little Sweep, a tale of innocence betrayed, from the first production by the English Opera Group in 1949. As well as being a landmark for Britten as a composer for children, this opera calls for audience participation in songs which act as interludes between the scenes. It looked forward almost ten years to the equally successful *Noye's Fludde*

compassion of the children of the house in which he is set to work, and the co-operation of their nurse, the boy is rescued from the clutches of his master and spirited away under the nose of the battleaxe of a housekeeper, to freedom and affection.

The Little Sweep would seem, from the number of times it has been performed, to be Britten's most popular opera so far. Its impact has been all the more important not only for the pleasure it gives in performance, but the way in which it has acted as a stimulus to music and opera in schools. This is surely a test of true inspiration.

For his next opera Britten turned to the sea. He chose a story by Herman Melville, *Billy Budd, Foretopman*, and E. M. Forster and Eric Crozier worked on the libretto together. *Albert Herring* had been dedicated to E. M. Forster, whose article on Crabbe had helped make up Britten's mind to return to England, and he was a devoted friend of the festival and Britten's music for the rest of his life.

It had been decided to hold a Festival of Britain in 1951, exactly a century after the Great Exhibition at the Crystal Palace, and in many ways this was intended to show the world that Britain was back on its feet again after the war. It was also a psychological spur to the country itself to speed up the long process of recovery. The Arts Council commissioned the opera

Noah's Ark, a relief in Framlingham Parish Church. When Britten decided to write another work for children in 1957 (*Noye's Fludde*), he went to the Chester Miracle play for his text, thus returning to a source he had originally tapped some five years previously in his setting of the Abraham and Isaac story (Canticle II), for alto, tenor and piano

Peter Pears as the young Essex and Joan Cross as the aged Gloriana in the original production of the opera at Covent Garden in June 1953. This was probably initially the least well received of all his operas, but the 1966 revival at Sadler's Wells did much to bring about a re-appraisal of its merits

from Britten for the festival, and at first it was intended that Sadler's Wells should present it at the Edinburgh Festival that year. It was soon evident, however, that the cost of mounting the opera would be beyond their resources, so *Billy Budd* was announced for Covent Garden for the autumn of 1951.

Britten began composing it in February 1950, and finished it in time for the announced opening, though he subsequently revised it in 1960. The first performance took place on 1 December 1951, with Britten conducting. John Piper designed the sets and Basil Coleman produced. The fact that it was known that there was an all-male cast had provoked some pessimistic comments beforehand, since the general run of operagoer tends to expect every opera to have its prima donna, but the performance revealed that Britten had created an amazingly wide variety of effects with the voices, as with the orchestration. Although he used a large orchestra for *Billy Budd*, he did not use it all for all of the time. Moreover, woodwind tends to dominate over strings, which means that the voices do not get swamped, and can hold their own. This is entirely consistent with Britten's theories of orchestration, and he himself has pointed out that it has not only been financial considerations that have dictated the sort of orchestra he has scored for at any given time. In Billy's Ballad in the Darbies, moreover, Britten has written one of his most beautiful pieces of music.

The theme of the opera is one of innocence betrayed, as indeed it was of *The Little Sweep*, but in *Billy Budd* the consequences are tragic. Instead of confronting the audience directly with the story, however, Britten presents it through the eyes of Captain Vere – the man who had the power of life and death over Billy – in the form of a Prologue and Epilogue.

The action takes place during the summer of 1797, on board HMS *Indomitable*. The ship is bound for the Mediterranean, and is short of men, so when a merchantman is sighted they board her and Billy Budd is taken from her crew. He is a handsome boy, but has a stammer at times. He gets on well with everyone on the *Indomitable*, apart from Claggart, the master-at-arms, who plots his downfall. Captain Vere sees through the plot, and brings Claggart and Billy together in his cabin. Billy is so amazed that he cannot reply, and he strikes Claggart dead. The captain summons a court at once, and Billy is sentenced to be hanged from the yardarm.

Much has been written about Britten's next opera, *Gloriana*, that has little to do with its merits as an opera. Not a little was inspired at the time by malice and envy. It was a relief to some people that Britten seemed at last to have come unstuck. To deal first with the extra-musical considerations, one has to recall the effects of the accession of Queen Elizabeth II. Coming a year after the Festival of Britain, and the desire to end the years of austerity, the country found itself with a young, beautiful queen called Elizabeth. There were inevitable comparisons with the glorious days of the first Elizabeth. People talked of a new Elizabethan Age, and mature men talked, in all seriousness, about being ready to die for their queen. The situation was dramatically pin-pointed when the queen went to dinner with her Prime Minister. There was something totally incongruous in that dazzling young figure on the steps of 10 Downing Street and the aged Winston Churchill, who was almost a relic of another epoch.

It was virtually inevitable, therefore, in such an atmosphere of unreality, that there should have been some disappointment with the story that Britten unfolded. It was not primarily a story of the glorious Queen Elizabeth I, but of an aged woman's infatuation for a younger man. Certainly she was shown as a queen, but also very much as a woman. Britten's treatment gave scope for pageantry – and a certain amount of pastiche – but the heart of the plot was the Elizabeth/Essex relationship. Possibly the material was not the most suitable for such an occasion, but in any case, the sort of audience gathered for a Coronation Gala at Covent Garden was hardly likely to be much concerned, or even particularly perceptive, about the merits of the opera itself.

Thanks to a new production at Sadler's Wells in 1966 it has been possible to re-appraise the work, and the general con-

An informal view of artistes at work. Benjamin Britten, Peter Pears, John and Myfanwy Piper and their two children, together with Basil Coleman the producer, have a picnic lunch on the steps of the little square behind the Fenice Theatre in Venice during the first performances of *The Turn of the Screw* in 1954

sensus seems to be that once all the extraneous considerations have been brushed aside, the work is a moving and touching exploration of its theme, though still a rather diffuse one. Sylvia Fisher has made the role of Queen Elizabeth I very much her own, though Joan Cross created it, and individual items such as the Earl of Essex' second lute song, the Choral Dances and the Courtly Dances, have won a place in their own right.

Britten had already been thinking about his next opera whilst busy with the composition of *Gloriana*. He had been commissioned to write an opera for the Venice Biennale of 1954 and he chose for it Henry James' story *The Turn of the Screw*. John Piper's wife, Myfanwy, provided the libretto, and in view of the smallness of the cast and the inclusion of children's voices, a return to the chamber opera format seemed indicated. The whole work is a very tightly knit essay by way of contrast with the expansive and, by comparison, rambling epic of *Gloriana*.

The story concerns two orphans, Miles who is eleven, and Flora who is eight, and is set in a country house, Bly, in Essex. The narrator is the children's new governess who, before coming to Bly, met their uncle and guardian in London and fell in love with him. Then the ghost of the uncle's valet, Quint, appears on the scene, and ultimately the Governess has to fight with the ghost for possession of Miles' soul. In the closing

section of the drama the Governess imagines that she has finally beaten Quint, but at that very moment Miles dies in her arms.

The Turn of the Screw has at its musical heart a rising note row, or basic pattern of notes on which the music is constructed, and a closely worked-out key sequence. The first does not determine the latter, however, since basically the keys ascend in the first act and descend in the second. In fact from a point of view of pure technique, this is one of Britten's most concentratedly technical operas. However, to say as much is not to do the work justice for the opera-goer, or tends to give the wrong impression. It is not an academic work to listen to. Pure technique is never preferred to auditory considerations.

As it happens the work contains one or two of Britten's most characteristic touches, such as the moving setting of Miles' mnemonic '*Malo, malo*, I would rather be', which is sung again by the Governess right at the end of the opera when he is dead. Britten also includes a popular tune, *Tom, Tom, the Piper's Son*, and gives it extended treatment to telling effect. Then there is the scene where the children sing a *Te Deum* or *Benedicite* on their way to church against the background of the bells, and interspersed with the text are words of their own. Another very typical Britten effect is the scene where Miles plays the piano in a more and more flamboyant way whilst Flora slips away to meet Miss Jessel, and by the end he is playing what is almost a triumphant toccata which forms the bridge or Variation (XIV) before the next, and penultimate, scene.

Despite a serious illness during the autumn of 1953, Britten was able to finish the score of *The Turn of the Screw* on time. In fact he started to write down the music left-handed, since his right shoulder was affected. He was well enough to conduct the first performance himself at Teatro la Fenice in Venice on 14 September 1954. John Piper again designed the sets and Basil Coleman produced.

After *The Turn of the Screw* there was to be what was, for Britten, a long interval before he wrote another opera. He naturally carried on composing and giving recitals, and the English Opera Group took *The Turn of the Screw* on tour during 1955. Then at the end of that year Britten and Pears went on a long tour through Yugoslavia and Turkey to Bali, Japan and India. This tour was to be the inspiration for some new works, in particular some of the music for the ballet *The Prince of the Pagodas*, and for a whole new kind of operatic venture, the parables for church performance. Britten had always intended that 1956 was to be a sabbatical year, with few concerts and recitals, though he went on composing, and it turned out to be a fruitful year in several respects.

When Britten finally settled down in Aldeburgh for the autumn of 1957 he decided to write a new children's opera. He had often thought of a successor to *The Little Sweep*. The stories of Beatrix Potter suggested a wealth of material, but there were problems about the copyright. Then in 1954 Britten and William Plomer, who had written the libretto for *Gloriana*, thought about a children's opera with space travel as its theme, but it is highly typical that when Britten did eventually decide on a new story, it should be taken from a medieval source, in fact from the Chester Miracle Plays, from which he had drawn the inspiration for his Canticle Abraham and Isaac, more than five years previously. It was at this time that Britten moved from Crabbe Street in Aldeburgh to the Red House, where he has lived ever since.

Noye's Fludde – for such was the title of the new work – turned out to be another Britten triumph. The theme of the corruption of innocence that had been a feature of so many of the previous works, with increasingly more sinister overtones in *The Turn of the Screw*, gave way to the simplicity and naïvety of a tale of forgiveness as seen through the medieval mind.

This version of the Biblical story of the Flood was to be an opera for children, in which children were to play the largest part. It was intended for performance in a church or similar large area but not, as the introduction to the score makes quite clear, a theatre. Britten consequently divided up the degree of skill expected from his amateur violinists, for example, into three categories. The third group was the most elementary, with a lot of notes written for the open strings. But here Britten's professional skill is once more apparent, for the open strings are not put in simply so as to make a virtue out of necessity. He puts them in where they are apt and fit the context precisely.

Another of Britten's touches, which he had used before – notably in *St Nicolas* – was to have the congregation join in hymns, but in *Noye's Fludde* the idea is much more effective. As the storm rises, the people in the ark begin to sing *Eternal Father, Strong to Save*, and all the audience join in with the

Opposite: The façade of the Teatro la Fenice, Venice, where Britten's opera *The Turn of the Screw* was given its première in the autumn of 1954. Apart from the very first opera, *Paul Bunyan*, which was performed in New York, this is the only one of Britten's operas to be given a first performance abroad, and Venice is one of the few places other than Aldeburgh where Britten is able to work

Overleaf: A dramatic moment from the original Covent Garden production of *Billy Budd* in 1951, showing the full muster of the crew on the main deck and quarter deck before Billy is hanged from the yardarm. The theme of the opera is again one of innocence betrayed, though on a much higher plane than that of *The Little Sweep*, and with the added dramatic and emotional impact of a full-scale opera

second verse. It is an incredibly moving moment, and in true Britten style gives a completely new look and significance to what was hitherto an old and probably too-familiar favourite. His version of the National Anthem is another perfect example of his great skill in this respect. The appearance of the rainbow in *Noye's Fludde*, greeted by a peal of handbells, and the use of a row of slung mugs on a line hit with a wooden spoon for the raindrops at the beginning of the storm, are the sort of effects we have come to expect from Britten, but this should not blind us to their originality, and the way in which he has enriched the repertoire of children's music and done so much to encourage and inspire their music making.

There are several purely technical touches in the opera, such as the fact that the tune used for the dove to fly off from the ark is reversed when the bird returns, and the storm is in fact a passacaglia, i.e. a bass theme constantly repeated throughout the passage, with the rest of the music constructed over it, which is one of Britten's – and Purcell's – favourite devices. But this does not affect the listener's approach to the music – except, perhaps, to increase his estimation of Britten's accomplishment. Similarly, the idea of having the animals sing *Kyrie eleison* (Lord, have mercy), as they pass into the ark, was entirely Britten's own idea, there was no indication of it in the Chester Miracle Plays.

To celebrate the completion of an enlarged stage and pit, and other general improvements to the Jubilee Hall at Aldeburgh, it was decided that Britten should write a full-length opera for the 1960 festival. Since time was short, and as Britten likes to work on a libretto that is more or less complete, he decided to take something that was already in existence, namely Shakespeare's *A Midsummer Night's Dream*, though the text had to be virtually halved in length. It was a play Britten had always liked, and he found the idea of the three basic groups of characters in the play, the Fairies, the Lovers and the Rustics, a challenge, and at the same time very suited to his kind of treatment.

In the opera he decided to use different groups of instruments for the various character groups. The Fairies have harps, harpsichord, celesta and percussion; the Lovers woodwind and strings; and the Rustics the lower brass and bassoon. The part of Puck is a speaking role for a child acrobat. Sometimes he has a trumpet and drum to accompany him, sometimes not. In preparation for the first French performance it was decided, with truly French logic, that an actor should be summoned from the *Comédie française* to play the part. When, in the course of the first rehearsal, the conductor gave the actor his cue for the first speech, he reacted with a look of total incomprehension when told that the words had to be spoken to a set number of bars and in strict rhythm.

Tytania and Oberon, really the chief characters in the opera, are written for coloratura soprano and counter-tenor respectively, which poses problems of balance in performance. There is also a casting problem, for counter-tenors are still an acquired taste in the opera house and tend so far to be confined mainly to England and America, with European countries following suit. Oberon may be played by a contralto, but the effect is not satisfactory. Coupled with the fact that the fairies are cast as treble voices, this makes one wonder whether the work will ever become a standard part of the repertoire.

There are some delightful moments in the opera, however, from the very first opening tremolo chords with upward and downward *portamenti*, which set the scene and impart a feeling of instability and otherworldliness, thus preparing one for what is to come. The fairy chorus that ends the first act 'On the ground sleep sound', in thirds over a rich chord of D flat, brings incredible peace and calm, especially as it returns to the words 'All shall be well'. The bewitching D flat chord occurs at one or two important points in the opera, for example just before Tytania, under Oberon's spell, professes her love for the disguised Bottom, 'O how I love thee'.

For sheer brilliance, however, the comedy of Pyramus and Thisbe, which becomes an opera within an opera, is hard to beat. Britten shows himself to be a master of styles – possibly including his own, since he seems at one point to be parodying himself – though the overall style of the episode is that of a 19th-century Romantic opera.

Britten wrote no more operas for four years, but in that time he wrote the *War Requiem, Cantata Misericordium, Sonata* in C for 'cello and piano, and the *Symphony* for 'cello and orchestra, as well as a *Jubilate* for St George's Chapel, Windsor Castle, a setting of *Psalm 150*, and *A Hymn of Saint Columba*. But in 1964 came a totally new kind of opera – a parable for church performance, as Britten described it – and there followed three in all, at two yearly intervals.

The first was *Curlew River*, in 1964, and the circumstances surrounding the initial genesis of a work can rarely have been

Rembrandt's painting *The Return of the Prodigal Son* in the Hermitage at Leningrad. This is one of the very few paintings that has directly inspired Britten to write a piece of music, in this case his third parable for church performance, in 1968. Although he had seen the painting some years previously, it was not until early 1968, in Venice, that Britten actually got down to the composition

A sadly ironic portrait of the poet Wilfred Owen in uniform. Britten included some of his poems in the text of the *War Requiem*, his telling testimony to the futility of war, and a work symbolic of reconciliation between countries formerly involved in two world wars

better documented. In addition to Britten's own programme note describing how he came to write the work, there is the diary of the late Prince of Hesse and the Rhine (1956), who accompanied Britten on the trip, parts of which are reproduced in the volume published for Britten's fiftieth birthday. Of the Japanese Nōh play that inspired *Curlew River*, the prince wrote at the time, somewhat cryptically: 'We feel that this is more than an interesting experience.' Eight years later he was proved right, for *Curlew River* was a totally new concept. Here is part of what Britten himself wrote.

'... The whole occasion made a tremendous impression upon me, the simple touching story, the economy of the style, the intense slowness of the action, the marvellous skill and control of the performers, the beautiful costumes, the mixture of chanting, speech, singing, which with the three instruments made up the strange music – it all offered a totally new "operatic" experience.

'There was no conductor – the instrumentalists sat on the stage, so did the chorus, and the chief characters made their entrance down a long ramp. The lighting was strictly non-theatrical. The cast was all male, the one female character wearing an exquisite mask which made no attempt to hide the male jowl beneath it.'

This might almost be the description of a performance of *Curlew River*, and yet Britten did not simply attempt to reproduce what he had seen in Tokyo. As he said in the same programme note, there was no question of making a pastiche opera inspired by the Japanese original which had so impressed him. He found his counterpart in England:

'Surely the Medieval Religious Drama in England would have had a comparable setting – an all-male cast of ecclesiastics – a simple austere staging in a church – a very limited instrumental accompaniment – a moral story?' And so it was that Britten moved from Japan to England, to a church in the Fens, but with a similar plot, that of a mother looking for her lost child. For music Japan had its centuries-old traditional music, and for a comparable musical source Britten took a plainsong hymn. He concluded: 'There is nothing specifically Japanese left in our Parable, but if we on the stage and you in the audience can achieve half the intensity and concentration of that original drama I shall be happy.'

Britten had written for churches, but not church operas solely for professionals. This is what makes the three church

Peter Pears as Nebuchadnezzar in *The Burning Fiery Furnace*. In all Britten has written three parables for church performance, as he calls them. They include a Japanese Noh play, an Old Testament story and a New Testament parable, but all are played within the framework of a medieval monastic convention, and take plainsong tunes for their thematic base

parables different. In some respects the idea may be traced back to *A Ceremony of Carols*, which dates from 1942. Certainly the idea of a Procession and Recession for the entry and exit of the performers is to be found there, and the medieval flavour of the carols is echoed in the setting of the scene with the monks processing on to the stage with plainsong, but once this is done, the three parables are very different. *Curlew River* transposes a Japanese medieval story into British medieval Fenland; *The Burning Fiery Furnace* takes an Old Testament story – that of the Three Holy Children; and *The Prodigal Son* takes the familiar New Testament parable and gives it a new look.

For all three parables William Plomer provided the libretti, and *Curlew River* was one of the few works that Britten has written away from Aldeburgh. It was written in Venice, a city he has always loved, and where he went in February 1964. He went there again in 1968, and a great part of *The Prodigal Son* was written there. This work is linked directly to a painting, namely Rembrandt's *The Return of the Prodigal*. He had seen it in the Hermitage in Leningrad, and decided to make that the theme of his next church parable.

Possibly the most novel aspect of the parables from a musical point of view is the fact that they dispense with a conductor. This means that vocalists and instrumentalists must be highly competent, and in close sympathy with each other. There must be a great deal of rehearsal also. Once more Britten devised almost a new style of music, in this case one that grew out of the plainsong which introduces each opera, and allowed a great amount of interplay between voices and instruments. The technique is something akin to that found in Balinese music, where the tune creates its own counterpoint, no matter how often it is superimposed on itself, or at what speed. The plainsong tunes provide something of the same effect, since they have fixed phrase length as far as the notes are concerned, a limited number of intervals, but great rhythmic freedom. Out of these specifically Christian settings, as befits performances in churches, flower the parables that are to be enacted.

It is difficult to see the church parable concept being repeated, though with Britten it is always possible that some new insight will lead him on to further developments. After the third parable, however, he turned his attention to television, and wrote the opera *Owen Wingrave* especially for the medium. It was originally commissioned by the BBC in 1967, but it was not until after *Peter Grimes* had been recorded for television at the Maltings, with Britten conducting, that he started composition. Britten wrote *Owen Wingrave* between September 1969 and March 1970. He is not especially a television fan, and the *Peter Grimes* recording doubtless helped him a great deal.

In his usual way he made an appraisal of the situation, and came to the following conclusion. 'I felt the main problem of TV opera was the choice of subject. One which made use of the intimate subtleties of the medium, including of course close-up shots which bring one closer to the singers than one can possibly be in the theatre. One which could use camera "abstractions" and of course quick scene changes and cuts, impossible or difficult on the opera stage. And one which didn't demand the impact of big crowd scenes and other "operatic" qualities of grand opera. I also wanted a subject which could be watched quietly at home, when the excitement of being part of a large audience in a theatre is not missed too much by the viewer.'

The subject Britten chose was a short story by Henry James, *Owen Wingrave*, and for his librettist he chose Myfanwy Piper, who had provided the libretto for the other James story, *The Turn of the Screw*. Perhaps more than in any other of his operas, Britten wrote for particular singers in *Owen Wingrave*. 'I wrote specifically for the particular singers not only for what I was sure they could do histrionically, but also for their particular vocal qualities.' As one might expect, there was a part for Peter Pears, but not that of the hero. He is sung in the opera by a baritone. The substance of the plot is a common Britten conflict, that of the individual in the midst of an unsympathetic society. To match the baritone of the hero, his fiancée in the opera is sung by a mezzo-soprano; in the first production Janet Baker in a somewhat unusual role for her.

The hero, Owen Wingrave, comes from a family with a long military tradition, but whilst he is at military school he realises that he cannot, in all conscience, become a soldier. The realisation and subsequent decision to give it up fills him with immense relief, but his family sees it only as an act of cowardice. He returns to the family home and his grandfather (sung originally by Peter Pears), fiancée and relatives, turn against him. There is a flashback to an earlier episode in the family history when a General Wingrave struck his son dead for refusing to fight a playmate, when challenged after a quarrel.

The General was subsequently found dead, with no apparent signs of injury. The room in which the incident took place is supposed to be haunted, and so as to prove that he is not a coward, Owen tells his fiancée that he will spend the night in the room. He falls a victim to the curse and is found dead.

In scope this opera stands somewhere between the full-scale operas and what are usually known as the chamber operas. Britten had initially envisaged a much smaller orchestra, and characteristically went to the trouble of finding out what instruments would sound best over the loudspeakers of the ordinary television set in the home. However, as the work progressed it seemed that a larger orchestra was called for, and there is conspicuous use of percussion in the score of *Owen Wingrave*.

Even before the work had gone out on television, however — which it did in May 1971 — Britten had decided to adapt it for the opera house. It was restricted to television for two years, however, but the fact that it has now been performed at Covent Garden leads one to conclude that there was nothing particularly different about writing for the medium on purely musical considerations, and certainly several of the existing operas have been televised without great difficulty from this point of view. The question is primarily one of production.

Britten's latest opera — an adaptation of Thomas Mann's *Death in Venice* — promises to be stimulating. There are only two principal singing characters, written for tenor and a baritone doubling several others parts. John Piper designed the sets and his wife Myfanwy adapted the libretto from Thomas Mann's novel of the same name. This opera represented a departure yet again, in that Britten introduced a lot of ballet, and in fact asked Sir Frederick Ashton, the former director of the Royal Ballet, to devise the choreography — particularly for the beach scenes.

It was inevitable that comparisons should have been made with Visconti's film, which was released more than a year before plans for the 1973 Aldeburgh Festival were announced, but Britten had begun work on his opera long before this. In any case, the identification of Aschenbach with Mahler in the film found no echo in Britten's conceptualisation of the role. Bearing in mind the long period of time that elapsed before *Gloriana* was adequately re-appraised, it will probably require a comparable interval before *Death in Venice* finds its appropriate place in the canon of operas.

Scenes from Britten's first television opera, *Owen Wingrave*, subsequently adapted for the stage and presented at Covent Garden in 1973. Benjamin Luxon was the hero, Owen Wingrave, and John Shirley-Quirk his tutor, Mr Coyle. Heather Harper was Mrs Coyle and Janet Baker Owen's fiancée, Kate. The theme of the opera, the individual taking his stand against family tradition, provided ample opportunity for dramatic situations, and takes up a theme already central to *Peter Grimes*

Opposite: A scene from the 1973 Aldeburgh production of *Death in Venice* with Peter Pears as Aschenbach and Robert Huguenin as Tadzio

Chapter Three
CONDUCTOR AND FESTIVAL DIRECTOR

The craftsmanship that went into the converting of the Maltings at Snape into a superb concert hall was not restricted to the building itself, and the excellent acoustics were heard to advantage at an early stage when Britten heard one of the workmen play his violin on the platform

THE idea of the Aldeburgh Festival came from Peter Pears as he and Britten were travelling from Holland to Switzerland with the English Opera Group in the summer of 1947. The cost of taking the operas on tour was crippling, and it seemed that at home, with friends, they should be able to put on their own festival. It was in 1947, of course, that the Edinburgh International Festival was launched, but there is a vast difference between Edinburgh and Aldeburgh.

To appreciate something of the significance that Aldeburgh has for Britten, and of the festival's place in his life, one has only to read what he said in his speech of acceptance of the Aspen Award in 1964: '... I belong at home – there – in Aldeburgh. I have tried to bring music *to* it in the shape of our local festival; and all the music I write comes *from* it. I believe in roots, in associations, in backgrounds, in personal relationships ... my music now has its roots in where I live and work ...'

In a way this might almost be taken as the statement of intent of the festival. For one thing, despite the stream of musicians, both British and foreign, who have been brought to Aldeburgh for the festival over the years, the festival has always been very conscious of its debt to Aldeburgh, and has always borne in mind its local character. In the winter of 1947, when Britten and Pears were back at home in Aldeburgh, they went first to the local people with their idea for a festival, and sought their co-operation. As Britten said when he received the freedom of the Borough of Aldeburgh in 1962: 'It is a considerable achievement, in this small Borough in England, that we run year after year a first-class Festival of the Arts, and we make a huge success of it. And when I say "we" I mean "we". This Festival couldn't be the work of just one, two or three people, or a board, or a council – it must be the corporate effort of a whole town.'

A glance at the festival programme of almost any year reveals how conscious the festival still is of its local roots. In 1967, for example, Rupert Bruce-Mitford lectured on Anglo-Saxon ship-burials and the Aldeburgh region in the 7th century, and the boys and girls of nearby Leiston Modern School gave a recital for Brass, Bells and Recorders. In 1968, the year of the twenty-first festival, in addition to the major concerts and an exhibition of paintings by Sydney Nolan directly inspired by Britten's cantata *Rejoice in the Lamb*, there were children dancing, a Punch and Judy show and bell-ringing.

This is one aspect, then, of the 'home' side of the festival. The other is the composer in residence, for he too is now a part of the 'home' side, and the festival has inspired a stream of works from him. The very first festival opened with *Saint Nicolas* (though it was in fact written for Lancing College that year), which was being heard for the very first time. E. M. Forster said of it: 'It was one of those triumphs outside the rules of art which only the great artist can achieve.' The first performance of *The Little Sweep* was in the Jubilee Hall in Aldeburgh in 1949, and the next two festivals saw two new works, *Lachrymae* for viola and piano in 1950 and *Six Metamorphoses after Ovid* for oboe in 1951, the latter given on the Mere at Thorpeness in an open-air concert. It was not until 1958, however, that another Britten première was heard at the festival, and that was *Songs from the Chinese*, followed next day by *Noye's Fludde*, which was given in Orford Church. It was also in Orford Church that the three parables for church performance were first heard.

For secular opera the Jubilee Hall in Aldeburgh itself did great service, but even when it was improved between the 1959 and 1960 festivals, it was obvious during the production of *A Midsummer Night's Dream* in 1960 that if the festival was to continue to produce opera, then a larger hall would have to be found.

In the meantime, a property was bought in Aldeburgh to serve as a Festival Club. Several people – artists and collectors included – donated works for auction, and Britten himself gave the autograph score of *The Young Person's Guide to the Orchestra* and initial sketches for *Seven Sonnets of Michelangelo*. The solution to the concert hall problem was found when it was decided to turn the old maltings at Snape, where Britten had once lived in a converted mill, into a concert hall. It was opened by Queen Elizabeth in 1967, and Britten wrote an overture, *The Building of the House*, for chorus and orchestra, for the occasion. In this new setting it was possible to mount a much less cramped production of *A Midsummer Night's Dream* that year. It was a great shock to everyone, therefore – even those who had only a vague idea of what Aldeburgh was all about – when the Maltings was burned down in 1969, with a superb grand piano and a great deal of equipment inside it. The festival that year had to be re-organised overnight, and it was that sort of determination that went into the rebuilding of the Maltings. Thanks to the efforts of all

Benjamin Britten, with Marion Stein (now Mrs Jeremy Thorpe) beside him, as pianist with the Amadeus Quartet in the 1952 Aldeburgh Festival

involved, a new and improved Maltings was open in record time. As the University Orator said in his speech at Cambridge when Peter Pears was made an honorary doctor in 1972: 'What faith they showed in immediately believing that their recently perfected concert hall, devastated by fire, could be restored, different yet the same, like the phoenix, and in accomplishing so great a task in a single year!'

It has also been the aim of the festival to bring other composers' music to it, or to bring into the public eye composers who have been neglected or forgotten. It is not surprising, therefore, that Frank Bridge and Purcell figure on the list, along with Britten's favourite composers: Mahler, Schubert, Mozart and Tchaikovsky. New works have also been commissioned. In 1953 *Variations on an Elizabethan Theme* – Selinger's Round – were heard for the first time. These were six variations on Byrd's original theme by Arthur Oldham, Michael Tippett, Lennox Berkeley, Britten himself, Humphrey Searle and William Walton.

Britten's friendship with Tippett is of long standing, and with Berkeley even longer. He is the only composer with whom he ever collaborated closely (on the *Mont Juic* suite), and Britten's *Piano Concerto* is dedicated to Berkeley. When the English Opera Group was re-launched in 1947, Berkeley's *Stabat Mater* was one of the two works commissioned that year by the group. To refer back to Britten's Aspen speech, he believes in associations, in backgrounds, in personal relationships, and it is this business of associations and relationships that has given the Aldeburgh Festival its special character.

Of course for those who do not enjoy a special relationship this may be offputting. There is no doubt that Britten is the artistic fulcrum of the festival, it revolves around him and he inspires it. At the same time, some people regret the atmosphere that they sense at times, of the festival being rather a closed shop. It was, however, essentially a festival of friends that Peter Pears originally envisaged, and there must be a limit to the number of friends one can claim to have.

One should be grateful that Britten has such talented friends, or has attracted talent to him, and that he has always been inspired by particular individuals to write some of his best music. The early *Phantasy* quartet is dedicated to the brilliant oboist Leon Goossens, who gave its first performance, and a much later work, *A Charm of Lullabies* (1947), was inspired by and dedicated to the mezzo-soprano Nancy Evans, who

The concert hall at nearby Snape, the Maltings, photographed at the end of June 1970, after it had been destroyed by fire and rebuilt

There have been many distinguished visitors to the Aldeburgh Festival since its inception. Here Benjamin Britten is seen with the famous Hungarian composer Zoltán Kodály (1882–1967). Britten chose one of Kodály's *Epigrams* (1954) as the theme for his *Gemini Variations*, written for a couple of Hungarian twin boy prodigies

One of the most fruitful and enduring relationships to have flourished at Aldeburgh is that between Britten and the Russian 'cellist Mstislav Rostropovich. They are seen here at the première of Britten's 'Cello Symphony given in the Moscow Conservatory in 1964. The première had been arranged for the 1963 Aldeburgh Festival, but had to be postponed because of Rostropovich's ill health at the time

sang the part of *Lucretia*, alternating with Kathleen Ferrier in the first performances. Once the festival got under way it seemed that a much closer involvement with particular talents became possible. In 1950 and 1951 it was the viola player William Primrose and the oboist Joy Boughton, who inspired the works mentioned previously for their respective instruments. *Canticle Two* (Abraham and Isaac) was written for the combined talents of Kathleen Ferrier, Peter Pears and Britten himself at the piano. The tragedy of Kathleen Ferrier's death robbed Britten of a voice ideally suited to his genius.

Another untimely death was that of the horn player Dennis Brain. He had given the first performance with Peter Pears of the *Serenade* in 1943, as well as that of *Canticle Three* (Still falls the Rain) with Pears and Britten in 1955. That particular work is dedicated to the pianist Noel Newton-Wood, who unfortunately had taken his own life.

Julian Bream, the guitarist and lutenist, was yet another individual talent to have inspired Britten. In 1957 Britten wrote a cycle of songs to Chinese lyrics, translated by Arthur Waley, for voice and guitar. Bream edited the guitar part and played it in the first performance with Peter Pears in the 1958 festival. Later, in 1964, Britten wrote a *Nocturnal* after John Dowland, for solo guitar, again for Bream. As an interesting piece of cross-fertilisation, Bream has arranged Britten's Courtly Dances from *Gloriana* for consort.

The following year, 1965, the song cycle *Songs and Proverbs of William Blake* was heard at the festival. This time the soloist was the distinguished German baritone Dietrich Fischer-Dieskau, who had sung the baritone solo in the first performance of *War Requiem* in 1962, and in *Cantata Misericordium* the following year.

More recently, of course, the most fertile relationship with a visiting musician has probably been with the Russian 'cellist Mstislav Rostropovich, and not only for the music that has been played and written, but because of the friendships that have been forged, and the bridge that has been made between Russian and British musicians and music in general. Britten has written a succession of works for Rostropovich, starting in 1961 with the *Sonata* in C for 'cello and piano (Op. 65); in 1963 the *Symphony* in D for 'cello and orchestra (Op. 68), which was to have had its first performance at Aldeburgh in that year, but eventually it took place in Moscow in 1964; and then in 1965 and 1967 respectively came the two *Suites* for 'cello, No. 1 in G (Op. 72) and No. 2 in D (Op. 80) with a third one in 1971. In 1964 Britten had also written a set of cadenzas for Haydn's *Concerto* in C for 'cello.

Britten met Rostropovich in London in 1960, and they agreed then that Britten would write a sonata for him. When he came to the festival the next year to give the first performance of the work, he also brought his wife, the soprano Galina

Benjamin Britten is an accomplished pianist in his own right. He has on occasions given joint performances with the Russian pianist Sviatoslav Richter, introduced to him in 1961 by Rostropovich

Britten with Dimitri Shostakovich in Moscow in 1963. As early as 1941, whilst reviewing Britten's opera *Paul Bunyan* in New York, Virgil Thomson had likened Britten's music to that of Shostakovich, but their friendship is of much more recent date, and they were in fact only introduced to each other in London in 1961 by Rostropovich

Vishnevskaya. Britten wanted her to sing the soprano part in *War Requiem*, but she was unable to do so because of previous engagements. It was also through Rostropovich that Britten met the pianist Sviatoslav Richter, in 1961, and he too became a regular visitor to the festival. Then in 1963 Britten and Pears were invited to Russia for a festival of British music, and the following year Britten conducted the postponed première of the *Symphony* for 'cello in Moscow. Shortly afterwards the first Russian performance of *Peter Grimes* was heard in concert version in Leningrad, and that autumn the English Opera Group took *The Rape of Lucretia*, *Albert Herring* and *The Turn of the Screw* on tour to Russia.

Further contact with Russia came the following year when Britten and Pears were invited to stay at a composers' home for creative work in Armenia, and then they went on to Yerevan for a Britten festival. Peter Pears kept a diary of this holiday which was privately printed in 1966, and he tells how they visited Pushkin's birthplace with Rostropovich and Vishnevskaya, and how a new Britten song cycle, *The Poet's Echo*, came into being, with settings of Pushkin's poems. Britten had bought a paperback edition of the poems at the airport on the way to Russia. There was another visit to Russia at the end of 1966.

The traffic between Aldeburgh and Russia was not all one way, however. In the 1967 festival a film of Shostakovich's opera *Katerina Ismailova* was shown (and again in 1968); Richter was the soloist and Britten the conductor in a performance of Mozart's *Piano Concerto* in E flat (K. 482), for which Britten wrote the cadenzas, and in Britten's own *Piano Concerto*, and Richter also gave a recital of Chopin and Debussy; there was a 'pictorial record' – *Russia Today* – by the photographer Burt Glinn, introduced by Laurens van der Post, and Britten, Pears and Richter combined to give a recital. The interesting feature was that Richter accompanied Pears in the vocal items instead of Britten.

In the twenty-first festival in 1968 there was again a strong Russian showing, with Rostropovich and Vishnevskaya, the Borodin String Quartet, and a fair amount of Shostakovich's music was performed. As an additional way of celebrating the festival's coming of age, Britten edited for subsequent publication *A Wealden Trio* for women's voices, which he had written in 1929, and also *The Sycamore Tree* (1930), for unaccompanied mixed voices. As well as indicating how much affection Britten has for his early music, these pieces serve to remind one of the essential part played by voices in Britten's work over the years.

Children's voices in particular have inspired some of Britten's most attractive music, and some of the earliest. They play an important part in *A Boy was Born* (Op. 3), and *Friday Afternoons* (Op. 7), 1934, was written for a school at Prestatyn

A caricature of Britten by Milein Cosman, wife of music critic Hans Keller, drawn in 1948, the year of the first Aldeburgh Festival

of which Britten's brother was headmaster. It consists of two volumes of songs – six in each – with piano accompaniment. The choice of the words is typical of Britten's wide-ranging eye for appropriate material, and is also a testimony to his knowledge of what is likely to appeal to children. There was also a group of part-songs, three in all, to poems by Walter de la Mare, which he wrote two years earlier, but since these are designated either for boys' or women's voices, they do not strictly speaking fall into this category.

In fact Britten did not fully exploit the idea of boys' voices until *A Ceremony of Carols* (Op. 28), 1942, which is related in some ways to *A Boy is Born*, and was a seminal work in several respects. It is in a way one of Britten's most typical works. He devised the idea of a Procession and Recession to begin and end the work, an idea he used again musically in the *Serenade* for tenor, horn and strings, where the horn has a solo Prologue and Epilogue at the beginning and end of the work. More important was the way in which Britten adapted it dramatically many years later, however, for his parables for church performance.

Another feature of *A Ceremony of Carols* was that Britten took an instrument that had been rather neglected previously, the harp, and gave it a new dimension. In this work it is called upon to provide a wide variety of different accompaniments for the voices, and then has a solo passage in the middle of the work. Finally, *A Ceremony of Carols* proved beyond doubt Britten's ability to get behind the feel of words and translate them into musical terms, and not simply set them to music. He has been particularly successful with medieval lyrics, and time and time again has used medieval material for his compositions. There is something in the immediacy and limpidity of the medieval mind that Britten appreciates readily, and is able to translate into contemporary terms.

The purity of treble voices obviously attracts Britten, and is part and parcel of his work for, and concern with, the education of the young in matters of music.

After *A Ceremony of Carols* Britten used boys' voices quite often. In *Rejoice in the Lamb* (Op. 30), 1943, there is a treble solo all about the cat Jeoffrey, and in *Saint Nicolas* (Op. 42), 1948, the whole work closely involves boys. *The Little Sweep* (Op. 45), written in the early part of 1949, uses boys' and girls' voices, and the *Spring Symphony* (Op. 44), written in the later part of 1949, despite the earlier opus number, not only has

Britten being greeted by the Jeney twins, Zoltán and Gabriel, for whom he wrote the *Gemini Variations*. He first met them in Budapest in the spring of 1964, and the work caters for their combined talents as pianists, flautist and violinist

boys singing with great gusto, but calls on them to whistle at one point also.

Children's voices figured again in *The Turn of the Screw* (Op. 54), 1954, and *A Midsummer Night's Dream* (Op. 64), 1960. It is interesting that opus 63, written round about the same time, is *Missa Brevis* in D, for George Malcolm and the boys of Westminster Cathedral Choir. Under George Malcolm the tone of the boys at Westminster became famous because of its 'continental' timbre, as opposed to what had always been regarded as the traditional English 'cathedral' tone. The fact that Britten had chosen to use the Copenhagen Boys' Choir (who came to sing in the 1952 Aldeburgh Festival) for an early recording that he conducted of *A Ceremony of Carols* leaves no doubt as to where his preference lay.

The *Missa Brevis* is occasional music, but it is not just a vehicle for showing off voices. Within its compact structure there are some beautiful vocal phrases to sing and some thrilling moments, too. There is both poignancy and urgent petition in the *Agnus Dei*, for example, with the yearning entries on the word '*Agnus*', which occurs three times, each time on a higher note, and closely written semitones for the voices in three parts on the words '*miserere nobis*'. Somehow Britten conveys the weight of sin on the word '*peccata*', with repeated falling quavers, two to each of the long '*a*'s in it. For '*dona nobis pacem*' Britten starts the voices piano and builds them up one on top of the other in strident semitones so that 'grant us peace' is not a pious prayer, but an insistent demand for peace. It dies away at the end, but not with a serene cadence, but a subdued muttering in the voices. The organ part has a rising ostinato pedal motif of one bar that is repeated twenty-one times throughout the movement, which makes it a kind of passacaglia, but the upper part of the organ score has clusters of semitones written frequently as a Scotch snap – a short note preceding a longer one – which might for all the world be car horns outside in Victoria Street in London, whilst the ritual of the Mass goes on inside the Cathedral. It is interesting that John Hahessey, who recorded *Canticle Two* (Abraham and Isaac) with Peter Pears and Britten at the piano, was also a chorister at Westminster Cathedral, though he now sings as the tenor, John Elwes. It was for him that Britten arranged Variation 5 of *A Boy was Born* as a solo, Corpus Christi Carol, in 1961.

It was almost inevitable that Britten should then write something for the greatest continental boys' choir, the Vienna Boys' Choir. However, they especially asked that they did not have to dress as girls, as they frequently are called upon to do when they perform operas, so Britten wrote for them the vaudeville *The Golden Vanity* (Op. 78) in 1966. It is a story of the sea, so they could all be jolly sailors.

They came to the 1967 festival to give two concerts, and *The Golden Vanity* formed the second half of the first one. The second half of the second concert consisted of *A Ceremony of Carols*. In this performance the harp was played by Osian Ellis, for whom the *Suite* in C for solo harp (Op. 83) was written in 1969. He gave the first performance of it at the festival that year, so continuing the tradition established over the years of new works first being heard at the festivals.

Boys' voices have also featured prominently in *War Requiem*, 1961; *Voices for Today* (Op. 75), 1965, and exclusively in the *Children's Crusade* (Op. 82), 1969, for the fiftieth anniversary of the Save the Children Fund. On this occasion the singers were the boys of Wandsworth School who, under their conductor Russell Burgess, have so successfully sung for Britten and provided him with the sort of tone he likes.

It is probably for the works conceived especially for children, however, or that most involve children, that Britten should be remembered with gratitude. First in chronological

As a conductor Britten has brought to his own works readings that will stand as guidelines for future generations as to their interpretation. This is not to suggest that these performances are necessarily definitive when they are captured on record, for Britten is a great believer in the individual performance of a work that makes it a unique occasion in the literal sense of the word. When it comes to the performance of other composers' works, then Britten brings to the scores deep sympathy and scrupulous attention to the composers' indications. Not all composers are so precise in conveying their intentions, however, as Britten is himself in his scores

sequence is *The Young Person's Guide to the Orchestra* (Op. 43), 1945, in which Britten not only provided an exciting way of getting to know the orchestra, but also brought back to the public's consciousness one of England's greatest, and then most neglected, of composers, Henry Purcell. Then must surely come *The Little Sweep* and *Noye's Fludde* (Op. 59), 1957. Kenneth Clark's words are eloquent enough in themselves to convey the impact of the work: 'To sit in Orford Church, where I had spent so many hours of my childhood dutifully awaiting some spark of divine fire, and then to receive it at last in the performance of *Noye's Fludde*, was an overwhelming experience. I heard the *Fludde* again at a rehearsal in Orford town hall ... and while the procession of Mice, Crows and Doves was being organised, I reflected on what it would have meant to me if, between the ages of nine and fifteen, such marvellous works of genius had been within reach ...'

On a smaller scale, but still doing the same work, is the setting of *Psalm 150* (Op. 67), 1962, followed in 1965 by the *Gemini Variations* (Op. 73). These were not written for beginners, however, but extremely gifted performers – even so, they were still children. This is how they came to be written. Britten was in Budapest early in 1964 and attended a music club meeting for children. There were some twins there, then aged twelve, both of whom played the piano, but in addition one played the flute and the other the violin. They also sang. At the end of the meeting they asked Britten to write something for them. They refused to accept as an excuse the fact that he said he was too busy, so he said that if they would write to him in English about their work, he would do so. Shortly afterwards the letter arrived, so Britten had to keep to his word and the result was the *Gemini Variations* on the theme of No. 4 of Kodály's *Epigrams* (1954). The twins came to Aldeburgh to give the first performance in 1965, and Kodály was in the audience. For less gifted individuals, the quartet may be performed by a quartet of players.

Other friendships revolve around Aldeburgh, not always musical, but essential to Britten's artistic life. There is Mary Potter, the artist, with whom he exchanged houses when he went to the Red House from Crabbe Street, and for whom he wrote the *Alpine Suite* for three recorders in 1955 when they were skiing at Zermatt and she hurt her leg. His relationship with the artist John Piper has been of long standing, Piper has designed many of Britten's operas for him, and Piper's wife

Myfanwy wrote the libretto of *The Turn of the Screw* and *Owen Wingrave*. *Winter Words* is dedicated to them.

Then there is the Earl of Harewood, who was president of the first festival. Britten wrote the wedding anthem *Amo ergo sum* for Lord Harewood's marriage to Miss Marion Stein in 1949. *Billy Budd* is dedicated to them, and it was whilst on a skiing holiday with the Harewoods in Austria that the idea of *Gloriana* was first discussed, in March 1952. *Winter Words* had its first performance at Harewood House in 1953 as part of the Leeds Festival, and *Nocturne* in 1958 in Leeds Town Hall for the Centenary Festival. Lord Harewood was the author of a perceptive article on Britten in a volume published in 1952, and also of a tribute to Erwin Stein (who had died in 1958) in the volume published in 1963 for Britten's fiftieth birthday.

The present Chairman of the Aldeburgh Festival Council is the Countess of Cranbrook, to whom *Cantata Misericordium* (1963) is dedicated. The Gathorne-Hardy children were the original children of *The Little Sweep*, and the family made two contributions to the fiftieth birthday volume. Robert Gathorne-Hardy wrote an essay entitled *Capriccio: Lathyrus Maritimus*

Britten with H.M. the Queen and the Duke of Edinburgh at the opening of the Maltings at Snape. The Queen returned for the opening concert in the hall after the fire

Overleaf: The conversion of the Maltings was carried out with immense sympathy for its environment, and little of the original exterior was lost in the process

Inset left: Britten in the charred ruins of the Maltings in June 1969, only two years after its completion. With characteristic determination, however, the festival went on that year, almost unaltered

Inset right: After the tragic inferno and the great artistic and financial loss, it might have seemed foolish to attempt to build again, but the decision was taken, and the restored hall was, if anything, better than the old one

(the Sea Pea), and the Earl of Cranbrook an essay on the Suffolk countryside. The Cranbrook home, Great Glemham House, has often opened its doors to the Aldeburgh Festival.

Britten's librettists have been of great importance to him, too; working associations sometimes developing out of friendships, or developing into them. Edward Sackville-West, E. M. Forster, Ronald Duncan, Eric Crozier, William Plomer and of course initially W. H. Auden, are names that spring to mind immediately.

But of all relationships, whether with artists or otherwise, it must surely be the relationship with Peter Pears – described by the Cambridge University Orator in 1959 as his *alter ego*, and in 1972 as 'the half of his soul' – that has so far produced the most sustained series of works. Starting with *Seven Sonnets of Michelangelo* (Op. 22) in 1940, there was subsequently the *Serenade* (Op. 31) in 1943, and the *Holy Sonnets of John Donne* (Op. 35) in 1945. In 1947 came *Canticle One*; in 1952 *Canticle Two* (with Kathleen Ferrier); 1953 saw *Winter Words* (Op. 52), and 1954 *Canticle Three* (with Dennis Brain). *Songs from the Chinese* (1957), did not involve Britten as accompanist, but exploited Pears' vocal technique, as did surely the *Six Hölderlin Fragments* (Op. 61) the following year, with Britten as accompanist once more. In addition to the more intimate works must be seen the long list of operatic roles, one in every opera with the exception of *The Little Sweep* and *Noye's Fludde*.

Naturally there are critics of Pears' voice, and no one could claim that it was what is usually regarded as operatic in style. But then operatic tenors do not always have the taste and intelligence that Pears brings to his music. It must have been of immense benefit to Britten to have someone to work so closely with, as indeed Schubert worked with Vogl. When Britten and Pears give a recital together one senses the marvellous working relationship that exists. As to how Britten might have evolved otherwise one cannot know. That must remain one of the 'ifs' of musical history.

In the same speech made in 1972, when Peter Pears was given a doctorate, one may read: 'But beyond all doubt he himself would value nothing so much as what he has achieved in partnership with "the half of his soul", Benjamin Britten, who, I am sure, would not mind my saying that his genius has to some extent been made by him: so many songs, so many roles, composed for him has he elicited from that source. It was he who first conceived the idea that an annual festival could be held at Aldeburgh in that corner of the earth dear to them both.'

In the shape of the Maltings, the Aldeburgh Festival had taken on an added dimension, though whether this is more rightly to be attributed to Britten himself or the Festival proper is impossible to decide. It has been used for antique dealers' fairs, jazz festivals, recording sessions, band concerts, and at certain times of the year there is sometimes a musical week-end which amounts to a little festival in itself.

Easter might be just such a week-end, and in 1972 Britten appeared as conductor in Bach's *St John Passion* on Good Friday. He approves of such performances, because Bach intended the work to be performed on that day of the year. Then the people present have come because they want to hear this particular performance. Some of them may have come quite a long distance, rather than hear it on the radio or put on a gramophone record. So the performance has all the ingredients for what Britten regards as a true musical occasion. It has the 'holy triangle of composer, performer and listener'. It also has Peter Pears as the Evangelist in an English version that has been maturing over the years, as he has gradually found the words that best suit Bach's original setting of the German.

Britten's interpretation of the *St John Passion* at present is taut and urgent. The swirling, restless quavers of the very opening bars and the piercing suspensions in the upper parts epitomise his reading of the work. The stupendous solace of the final chorus is yet to come. The Wandsworth School boys' choir with its bright, piercing tone and incisive attack is exactly the instrument he wants for the crowd parts. Like the crowd in *Peter Grimes*, the crowd of the *St John Passion* plays a crucial part in this particular story.

Then on the Sunday afternoon we hear a chamber concert with Britten as pianist in the Schumann piano quartet, and then as accompanist to Pears in the *Holy Sonnets of John Donne* – a difficult work to perform, and therefore all the more reason to relish this performance. Sandwiched between the two concerts is a programme of Bach and Vivaldi concertos on the Saturday evening. Perhaps even more than the festival itself, a week-end at the Maltings shows the quintessence of the musical world of Britten and Pears – '...how harmoniously they combine to produce divine sounds, what rich feasts of music they devise together!'

Chapter Four
COMPOSING FOR THE VOICE

Boys' voices have inspired some of Britten's most successful works. Here he is seen with the score of *The Golden Vanity* talking to its performers at Aldeburgh. It was originally written for the Vienna Boys' Choir, who especially asked for a costume piece in which they would not have to dress as girls. The result was a vaudeville with a nautical flavour

Below: Britten in Moscow with the Russian soprano Galina Vishnevskaya, wife of the 'cellist Rostropovich. Britten very much wanted her to sing the soprano part in his *War Requiem*, but she was unable to do so

Bottom: Britten with Tyrone Guthrie, with whom he collaborated on a realisation of Gay's *The Beggar's Opera* in 1948 at the Arts Theatre in Cambridge. Three years later followed another realisation, Purcell's *Dido and Aeneas*

WHEN once asked whether vocal or instrumental composition presented him with the fewest problems, Britten replied that composition is never easy, the problems are simply different. By sheer volume of vocal writing, however, one might be forgiven for thinking that he prefers writing for voices. Indeed, Britten's earliest published work – which is also one of his favourites – is a song with piano accompaniment, *The Birds*, dedicated to his mother. It was written at Holt, in Norfolk, in 1929 and was revised five years later. Since 1966 Britten has edited and published more of his early music, though his Opus 1 is still the *Sinfonietta* for chamber orchestra, 1932, which is dedicated to Frank Bridge. It is clear, then, that from the start he was strongly attracted to vocal music, and in his last term at his preparatory school he set a group of four French songs for soprano solo and orchestra, the full score of which still exists. As David Willcocks, conductor of the Bach Choir and Principal-designate of the Royal College of Music has said, '... he seems to have an uncanny knowledge of what the human voice can do and of how best to exploit its many features'.

Britten understands the singer's problems and does his best to help him, without in any way compromising his own integrity as a composer. During the rehearsals for *Canticle Four* (The Journey of the Magi), Britten realised that a particular phrase did not lie well for the top voice, and so adjusted it accordingly. Much of the revision carried out on *A Boy was Born* (Op. 3), in 1955, was to make it a better work to sing, as well as to listen to, but Britten has never written down to his singers. This is a process which works both ways, because if a singer finds a particular phrase uncomfortable or difficult, and the composer is either intractable or, on the other hand, asks the singer what he would prefer – which has happened often in contemporary music – then the singer loses respect for both the composer and his music, and the pleasure and satisfaction of performance is lost.

When writing to commission, Britten takes great care to find out as much as possible about the nature of the occasion, the forces available, and their standard of musicianship. He then elaborates his conception accordingly. Even so, he has almost always seemed to have been able to draw something out of his performers – and this is especially true of his writing for amateurs – that took them a little further than their assumed limitations, and in this way he has done an immense amount to improve musical standards. On the other hand, there is no

A study of Britten at the piano in 1946, the year which saw *The Rape of Lucretia*, *The Young Person's Guide to the Orchestra*, completed on New Year's Eve, and the Occasional Overture in C for the opening of the BBC Third Programme (a work he subsequently withdrew)

doubt that some of his best vocal music, especially some of the songs written with Pears in mind, is also among his most difficult. But whatever the context, Britten always writes vocally for singers – 'gratefully' is his own word – unlike many contemporary composers, whose voice parts often seem more suitable, in their demands for agility and range, for instruments.

In addition to his understanding of the human voice, Britten has an amazing facility for setting words which, paradoxically, may pose problems for a librettist. Myfanwy Piper has written: 'Britten's way of using the human voice is at once a marvel and a problem for the librettist. This I knew long before there was any question of becoming one myself. A marvel because of his passionate respect and love for words and a problem because every single word is set to be heard, not only for its part in the story but for its quality as part of the human instrument.'

Although Britten does not claim to be a linguist, he nevertheless has a strong feeling for languages, and has set French, Italian, Latin, German and Russian texts. His sensitivity to language was revealed in an interview with Murray Schafer when he said that he had made one or two small mistakes in the setting of the words of *Les Illuminations* (Op. 18), but that only English people had bothered to point out such a thing to him, the French had not minded. Elsewhere he said that he had had some problems with the Latin quantities in the words of *Cantata Academica* (Op. 62).

When it came to another Latin text, this time for *Cantata Misericordium*, Patrick Wilkinson his librettist for the work, who is a fellow of King's College, Cambridge, and University Orator, gave Britten a private lesson in his rooms in the college on quantities and accents before he began, and then later went to stay at Aldeburgh, and Britten played passages over to him on the piano. In fact Britten errs on the side of modesty when he says that he is not a linguist, and he is extremely sensitive to translations of his words. He is not very satisfied, for example, with the German translation of his opera *A Midsummer Night's Dream*, and the French translation leaves a lot to be desired.

This sensitivity in the setting of words to music is fundamental to Britten's art, and has produced an apparently endless stream of flashes of genius. The declamatory treatment in *Les Illuminations* of the sentence '*J'ai seul la clef de cette parade sauvage*' (I alone have the key to this wild parade), which

Although Britten has at times scored for the harpsichord to great effect, it is not an instrument he has specialised in at all. This harpsichord at Aldeburgh was made in 1953 by Alec Hodsdon of Lavenham in Suffolk

becomes almost literally the key to the cycle, is one such example where Britten has found the perfect setting of the words, but one finds examples throughout his music. In a very different context, for example, is the pleading voice of Sammy in *The Little Sweep* (Op. 45) singing 'Please don't send me up again', with falling semitones, and all the other children joining in with a determined 'We won't send you up again', rising defiantly to end on a triumphant major chord.

This is not to say that there are never any weak moments at all, and some of Britten's effects may seem – in retrospect – a little obvious, such as the treatment of the word 'dying' in the Nocturne from the *Serenade* (Op. 31) for tenor, horn and strings. Then at the moment in *Peter Grimes* (Op. 33) when Ellen discovers that Peter has started maltreating the new apprentice, she is given the words 'A bruise... well it's begun!' Britten sets the first word to a B natural, rising to an F sharp for the word 'bruise'. At first hearing, the effect does not convey the alarm and despair that Ellen feels, because of the way stress is given to a word – 'bruise' – that is usually so banal in connotation. But this is to strain at gnats when there are so many other things that ring in the mind long after the performance has ended. Britten himself has said that this passage gave him trouble, but in the context of the opera as a whole, the scene works dramatically.

Another example, more strictly concerned with the matching of music and words, is provided by the last carol '*Deo gracias*' from *A Ceremony of Carols* (Op. 28). After an initial arpeggio from the harp, the opening phrase '*Deo gracias*' is set to an energetic, fanfare-like phrase of leaving intervals and sharp, rhythmic effects that underlines the joyful and vigorous exclamation of the words, 'Thanks be to God'. Then comes a series of staccato quavers, all on the same repeated notes, with the three voices together in thirds, for the words 'Adam lay ibounden'. Britten has found the exact musical form once again to capture the clipped vowels and percussive consonants of those words. So the carol runs on, with frequent syncopation in the voices against insistent quaver passages on the harp, and then swooping arpeggios to bring back the voices with their cries of '*Deo gracias*'. When the singers come to the words 'Blessèd be the time/That appil takè was', there is a dramatic switch from minor to major, and the carol ends in a riot of entries of '*Deo gracias*', in three-part canon, with glissandi on the harp.

For an example of Britten's word setting at its most unorthodox, and yet in the event equally successful, one might take the closing chorus of fairies in *A Midsummer Night's Dream*, which begins with the words 'Now until the break of day'. Britten makes the syllables that are weak in the spoken verse three times longer than the strong ones (when spoken), because in the music he sets them to a series of Scotch snaps. Even so, Shakespeare's original overall accentuation is not lost, because Britten's setting is in 4/4 time, and the strong beats of the bar fall naturally on 'Now' and 'break' which is where they fall in the spoken verse, too.

With such sensitivity in the setting of words it would be surprising if, when it came to performance, Britten were not equally sensitive as a pianist, and indeed much has been said about his skill as an accompanist. Were he not a composer, he would almost certainly have established himself with a world-wide reputation as an accompanist, or even as a concert pianist, in his own right. In fact Britten was the soloist in the first performance of his own *Piano Concerto* (Op. 13), with Sir Henry Wood in London in 1938.

Clifford Curzon paid tribute to his skill in a book published to celebrate Britten's fiftieth birthday in 1963. 'More than anything else, of course, I wish I could find words of my own to describe the unique impression of your superb piano playing; but it seems to defy all ordinary analysis. The complete mastery with which you dispose amounts and kinds of orchestrally-inspired tone would be as difficult for me to describe as Beethoven's volcanic playing apparently was for *his* contemporaries...' After hearing Britten accompany Pears in a recital, Francis Poulenc, who had a similar partnership with singer Pierre Bernac, said that he would stop playing Schubert forthwith.

Other singers who have had the good fortune to experience this wonderful playing, when being accompanied by Britten, agree unanimously about his skill. Indeed really good accompanists are by no means easy to come by. Of course, like any other performer, Britten may be nervous or ill at ease before a concert if he is not totally satisfied with arrangements, but when things go well – as they do most of the time – then Britten is undoubtedly in total control.

Rostropovich, in a moving article that he contributed to the fiftieth birthday volume, tells how he went to Aldeburgh with his wife and rehearsed with Britten the programme of a concert they were to give together. It was to include Schubert's Sonata, which he had never played before, and in fact only began to learn a few days before the actual concert. He was amazed at Britten's capacity and energy for work, and his concern for even the slightest detail, but he was even more amazed by the way in which Britten accompanied him in the newly learned sonata.

'Some of the difficult spots tripped me up at the rehearsal. Britten, of course, noticed them immediately. It was indeed something to see and hear: when we approached the spots in the Sonata that were risky for me he tried to make it easier. He'd slow down somewhat, putting me in a cradle, so to say. He placed such a fine piano cradle under the 'cello part that I was able to play all the notes that were there without panicking.'

One must also bear in mind the fact that Rostropovich does not only see things from the 'cellist's point of view. He is also an accomplished pianist in his own right, and often accompanies his wife in recital. This gives Britten and Rostropovich yet another area of common ground.

For a composer who has done so much for amateur music-making, and has always seemed an essentially English musician, it may perhaps seem surprising that folksong has not played a larger part in Britten's music. There are of course the six books of folksong arrangements (mainly for voice and piano, with one volume for voice and guitar), which have many characteristic Britten touches. Eight of the British songs are orchestrated, as well as six of the French.

In the orchestrated version of *The Ploughboy*, for example, Britten gives a very sprightly accompanying tune to the piccolo, and the rest of the accompaniment is confined to the strings, or in *The Salley Gardens* a plaintive counter-tune – based on the voice part – is given to the bassoon in the accompaniment, with harp and strings. But to hear Britten accompany Pears when they are performing the piano version, one might think that he had the instruments there at his command.

In his arrangement of the Welsh folk song *The Ash Grove*, which is for piano only, Britten uses a Welsh tradition known as *Penillion*, in which the singer plays a traditional tune, usually on a harp, and sings his own improvised counter-melody against it. In the Britten arrangement the singer sticks to the original tune whilst the piano provides the alternative

Peter Pears is an international soloist in his own right, and often appears outside the Aldeburgh Festival, both at home and abroad. Here he is seen studying a score with Britten in his London studio

melody, which is partially an echo of the tune, but so as to underline the poignancy of the words of the second verse, Britten moves the accompaniment chromatically, often with octave leaps and, at the climax, octaves in the right hand. The psychological insight into the words that Britten conveys would be admirably suited to an art-song, but for a folk song seems more profound than the original is able to bear. A similar treatment, and one which in its context is much more successful, is used for the French folksong *Quand j'étais chez mon père*. Even so, the accompaniments to all these songs are full of sensitive moments, and suggest a wealth of experience in the art of accompanying the voice.

For a composer so concerned with voices, and boys' voices in particular, it is not surprising that Britten has given the Church of England some striking additions to its repertoire. Here again, however, one sees in operation the spirit that caused Britten to stop writing music for sound tracks and plays and choose his own libretto when he wanted to set words. In that way, he would be sure of being in on the work from the start. He has not, therefore, set traditional texts such as the canticles, apart from a *Te Deum* in C major, 1935, which was provided with a complementary *Jubilate* – at the request of the Duke of Edinburgh – in 1961. The 1935 *Te Deum* has a very lively syncopated pedal part, and much of the voice part consists of fanfare-like arpeggios up and down the chord of C major. There is a treble solo in the middle section, with one or two beautiful moments when the solo voice is left on a long top note and the other voices fall away, then the solo voice descends in an echo-like effect. It was doubtless purely by accident, but Sir William Walton used this very effect at one point in his *Te Deum* written for the queen's coronation in 1953.

When the 1935 *Te Deum* was performed at the Mercury Theatre in London in January 1936, Constant Lambert went along to hear it and review it for *The Sunday Referee*. He did not find the work much to his taste. 'Mr Britten is, I admit, rather a problem to me. One cannot but admire his extremely mature and economic methods, yet the rather drab and penitential content of his music leaves me quite unmoved.' The effect of the *Te Deum* nowadays is scarcely likely to be 'drab and penitential', though it might well still shock people with very hard and fast ideas about church music. However, Lambert went on, 'At the same time he is the most outstanding talent of his generation and I would always go to hear any first performance of his.'

In view of this opinion, it would be interesting to know whether Lambert ever saw the ballet score which Britten submitted to the Camargo Society, of which Lambert was the conductor, four years previously, in 1932. The score was returned to Britten and was never performed. It might possibly have set him on the road to fame a little earlier had it been otherwise.

The second *Te Deum* in E major (Op. 32), dates from 1945. It is conceived in a very different way, with the organ part barred completely independently of the voice parts, which are scored in unison for much of the work. In both these settings, however, Britten shows a freshness of approach that was previously shown only by such composers as Vaughan Williams and Holst in his Short Festival *Te Deum* of 1920. Between the Britten *Te Deum* of 1945 and the *Jubilate* of 1961 there had been many innovations in Anglican church music, but his treatment of the text of the later canticle as alternate passages of rather angular unison dialogue and subdued close harmony for the voices, against a sparkling, bouncing tune for the organ, was a flash of genius. There was again verbal unorthodoxy, too, for in the final 'Amen' Britten has written the Amens in pairs and misplaced the stress, so that the heavy beat falls on the first 'A', whereas the stress is usually either equally divided between both syllables or, if anything, heavier on the 'men'.

Nevertheless it would be fair to say that Britten's happiest inspirations in the realm of church music have been stimulated when he has been able to choose his own texts. One of his very earliest works is still one of his most captivating, *A Hymn to the Virgin*, written in his last year at school in 1930, and revised in 1934. He was in the school sick bay at the time, and there was no manuscript paper to hand, so he ruled the lines of the stave on a page from an exercise book. The text is an anonymous medieval hymn *circa* 1300, in which the lines alternate between Latin and English. Britten divides his singers into two, and has one choir sing the English and one the Latin. The idea is perhaps obvious in retrospect, but most effective.

During the winter of 1932–3, Britten wrote a set of choral variations, dedicated to his father, which he revised in 1955, *A Boy was Born* (Op. 3). Imogen Holst has pointed out that, had Britten been able to have his works performed whilst he was

Imogen Holst, photographed here in 1926, is the daughter of the composer Gustav Holst (1874–1934), and one of the artistic directors of the Aldeburgh Festival since 1956. She and Britten have worked together on performing editions of *Dido and Aeneas*, *The Fairy Queen*, and a book, *The Story of Music*. For a long time she helped him prepare the scores of his works for performance

still a student, he might have avoided some of the original problems in the work, and not had to revise it. The theme, from which the work takes its title, is an anonymous 16th-century carol, and the six variations are all poems on the birth of Christ. *A Boy was Born* is not necessarily church music, despite the religious theme, but it showed how, at an early age, Britten was to respond to words, and piece texts from widely differing sources into one cohesive work.

The next work that can be said to have a religious theme is the *Hymn to St Cecilia* (Op. 27), of 1942. The text is by Auden, and no one would say that the work as a whole conveyed any specifically religious atmosphere. It is much more akin to the odes that Purcell and Handel wrote for St Cecilia's Day and various royal occasions, and in writing his 'Hymn' to St Cecilia, Britten was both honouring his patron saint and at the same time reviving an old tradition. In the Purcellian ode the slightest mention of a musical instrument was the cue for the composer to bring in the instrument in question. Thus one solo might be accompanied by violins as solo instrument, and the next one by flutes. Britten pays more than a passing tribute to the convention in his *Hymn to St Cecilia* when he writes a series of short cadenzas for each voice part in turn, imitating successively the violin, drum, flute and trumpet.

Another work written at exactly the same time, on the voyage back to England from America, does, however, convey a religious atmosphere, and that is *A Ceremony of Carols* (Op. 28). Possibly the fact that it is for treble voices, with words of medieval carols, associates it more readily with churches, but a clue surely lies in the word 'ceremony' of the title. The work almost has a liturgical character, as if Britten had invented a new act of worship. This is heightened by the plainsong Procession and Recession, which set the scene, so to speak, for the ceremony, and then conclude it. Britten returned to this idea – via the Japanese Nō theatre – some twenty-two years later with the parable for church performance *Curlew River* (Op. 71). In the later work he also uses plainsong, and moreover uses it thematically in the subsequent music.

The use of the harp in *A Ceremony of Carols* was another of Britten's strokes of genius. Though harps may have been used in churches from time to time in the Middle Ages, there is no established tradition for their use. In *A Ceremony of Carols* it seems hard for any other instrument to have been envisaged. Moreover, Britten exploits the inherent qualities of the instrument, as in the *allegro* opening to the first carol 'Wolcum Yole!', which is marked *pesante ed arpeggiando*, and the glittering, frosty triplets in the upper register for the central section. Although Britten wrote so brilliantly for the harp in this work, it was not until 1969 that he published another work for the instrument, the *Suite* in C (Op. 83), though he has scored for it to great effect in, for example, *A Midsummer Night's Dream*.

Britten's flair for choosing and setting words was given a further opportunity for expression when he was asked to write something for the fiftieth anniversary of the consecration of St Matthew's Church, Northampton, in 1943. The incumbent, Walter Hussey (subsequently Dean of Chichester), had commissioned a *Madonna and Child* from Henry Moore and a mural of the *Crucifixion* from Graham Sutherland. Britten wrote a Festival Cantata, *Rejoice in the Lamb* (Op. 30), to words by the 18th-century poet Christopher Smart, who was very religious, but who was in a lunatic asylum at the time he wrote the poem from which Britten's work takes its title. Within its comparatively short length, there is a wealth of invention. There is a beautiful tenor solo about the flowers; an amusing solo for alto about a mouse; the treble sings about his cat Jeoffrey, who worships God in his way 'by wreathing his body seven times round with elegant quickness', and the chorus has a lively tune in alternating 7/8 and 6/8 time for 'Let Nimrod, the mighty hunter, bind a leopard to the altar and consecrate his spear to the Lord'. But possibly the most poignant moment in the whole work is the repeated shout of 'Silly Fellow' that Britten sets for the chorus to a bitterly chromatic figure, and could well be the voice of Smart himself. One thinks inevitably of the moment in *Peter Grimes* when the crowd is heard shouting Peter's name, and he then goes into a long vocalisation of his name that is a cry from the very depths of his being.

Three years later Britten wrote another work for St Matthew's, Northampton, this time for the church's patronal festival, and it was a Prelude and Fugue for organ on a Theme of Vittoria.

Rejoice in the Lamb established a pattern for some of the church music that Britten wrote subsequently, but the cantata *St Nicolas* (Op. 42), which was written for the centenary of Lancing College in 1948, envisaged much larger forces than its predecessor. For one thing, larger forces were available than there had been for *Rejoice in the Lamb*. In fact it was a landmark for the future. It was used to open the first Aldeburgh Festival in 1948, and its effect was stunning. Two hymns were included, so that the congregation could join in, and this made it eminently suitable for use in churches. In this respect it looked forward to *Noye's Fludde* (Op. 59) by some ten years. There is also a storm at sea in *St Nicolas* and a flood – The Flood, in fact – in *Noye's Fludde*. But one of the most magic moments in *St Nicolas* is again one of Britten's touches of genius. The scene dealing with the saint's birth and childhood is set to a lively waltz tune with the words 'Nicolas was born in answer to prayer, And leaping from his mother's womb he cried:' There is a long crescendo marked in the voice part on the word 'cried', but the organ comes in with a *pianissimo* chord, and a treble voice is heard singing 'God be glorified'. In the last verse, when Nicolas leaves his childhood, the treble voice is suddenly transformed into a rich tenor as the soloist takes over. In its way it is similar to the ease with which Shakespeare can completely change the scene in two lines of poetry, without anything actually having happened at all. So in *Hamlet*, when the opening scene on the battlements draws to its close, Horatio speaks: 'But, look, the morn, in russett mantle clad, walks o'er the dew of yon high eastern hill.'

We are then swiftly taken into the interior of the castle.

Two further anniversaries, the quincentenary of St Peter Mancroft, Norwich, in 1955, and the centenary of St Michael's College, Tenbury, the following year, produced respectively *Hymn to St Peter*, with words from the gradual for the feast of St Peter and St Paul, and *Antiphon*, a setting of George Herbert's poem. They are designated Op. 56a and b. After this there was a gap until 1959 with *Missa Brevis* in D (Op. 63), which is the only music Britten has written specifically for the Roman liturgy, and then came the Anglican *Jubilate* of 1961.

In 1962, Britten's old preparatory school celebrated its centenary, and he set *Psalm* 150 (Op. 67) for two-part children's voices, with instrumental parts that they could play. Later that year he wrote *A Hymn of St Columba* for the fourteenth centenary of the saint's journey from Ireland to Iona, which returned to the forces used for the earlier hymns and cantatas, namely four-part mixed chorus and organ.

It is difficult to know which of the two is more deeply seated in him, either Britten's flair for choosing the best words to set,

Below: Henry Moore's statue of the Madonna and Child in St Matthew's Church, Northampton, for which Britten was commissioned to write the festival cantata *Rejoice in the Lamb* in 1943

Top right: Graham Sutherland's mural of the Crucifixion, also in St Matthew's Church, Northampton. Britten wrote a second work for the church, a prelude and fugue for organ on a theme by Vittoria, the Spanish composer

Below right: For the 1968 festival, the Australian artist Sidney Nolan painted a series of pictures of which this is one directly inspired by Britten's setting of *Rejoice in the Lamb*, in the way that he had also been inspired by Britten's setting of Thomas Hardy's *Winter Words*

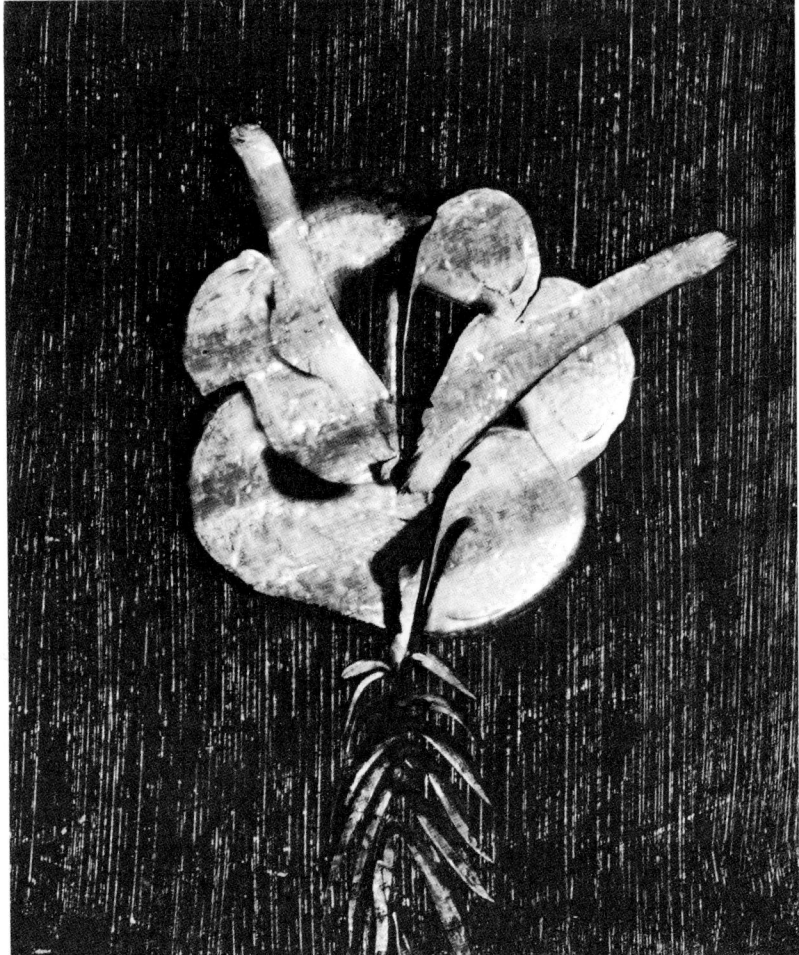

Britten, with Rostropovich and Vishnevskaya, acknowledges the applause after a concert at Yerevan in Russia, in September 1965. A festival of his music opened on 28 August, and it was there that two extracts from a new song cycle to words by Pushkin, *The Poet's Echo*, were first heard

Britten, with Rostropovich and Peter Pears beside him, receives a gift of a painting, *A Sunny Day*, by the Armenian artist Martiros Saryan after a concert of the Yerevan festival in 1965

or his innate feeling for what is vocally right. He has always seemed to respond instinctively to words, and it was fascinating, in this respect, to see the list of poems that he chose for a BBC programme 'Personal Choice' in 1958, since all the poems he chose had not then been set to music – by Britten at least. Some of the items he was eventually to set, in particular Wilfred Owen's *Strange Meeting* in the *War Requiem*, but it gives an insight into the way Britten may store up things in his mind, sometimes for years on end.

On the other hand, he may also react spontaneously to a situation, as in the case of the Pushkin poems that became *The Poet's Echo* (Op. 76). The genesis of this song cycle is particularly fascinating in this respect. On the way to the airport for a trip to Russia in 1965, Britten bought a paperback copy of Pushkin's poems with the English translation at the bottom of the page. So as to improve his Russian he decided to set some of them to music. He got Rostropovich and Vishnevskaya to read the correct Russian pronunciation to him. Before they left Armenia where they had been staying, the songs had all been sketched out. Later, when motoring from Novgorod to Leningrad, they made a visit to Pushkin's home. Peter Pears has described this visit in his privately printed *Armenian Holiday*. They did not reach the place until eight o'clock in the evening, which was a day later than expected. Their hosts had waited for them all night, and Rostropovich had not telephoned to warn them that they would be late. However, they were greeted as if nothing at all had happened. Pears then went on:

'The quiet was extraordinary; there were lilac-bushes brushing the gutters, the beds of white phlox along the garden paths filled the Library with scent ... our host took a torch and showed us Pushkin's house and museum, and outside the front door was the clock tower and its cracked clock which was there in Pushkin's time and still struck its old hours.'

Their host had obviously been told that Britten had set some Pushkin poems to music, for he asked if he could hear them. When they had eaten, Britten agreed.

'We moved into the lamp-lit sitting-room with an upright piano in the corner, and started on the songs (after an introduction by Slava [Rostropovich]). Galya [Vishnevskaya] sang her two, and I hummed the others. The last song of the set is the marvellous poem of insomnia, the ticking clock, persistent night-noises and the poet's cry for a meaning in them. Ben had started this with repeated staccato notes high-low high-low on the piano. Hardly had the little old piano begun its dry tick-tock tick-tock, than clear and silvery outside the window, a yard from our heads, came ding, ding, ding, not loud but clear, Pushkin's clock joining in his song. It seemed to strike far more than midnight, to go on all through the song, and afterwards we sat spell-bound. It was the most natural thing to have happened, and yet unique, astonishing, wonderful.'

The Poet's Echo is described as 'a dialogue between the poet and the unresponsiveness of the natural world he describes'. The way it happened in Russia, one would say that the natural world had not been unresponsive. Sometimes similar things have happened much nearer home, in Blythburgh Church, for example, during the 1967 festival. The programme consisted only of two works, Heinrich Schütz' *The Seven Last Words upon the Cross* and *The Resurrection Story*. The music was not Britten's, but Peter Pears was the first tenor soloist. It was a warm summer's afternoon, but as the story of the Passion was told, and Schütz' music became more intense, the sky darkened and a huge storm loomed up and then broke. At one point it seemed as if the performance might have to be interrupted until the storm abated. But the Passion went on, and the storm passed. *The Resurrection Story* was sung, after the interval, in bright sunshine, and the Evangelist joined with the choir in the closing moments with cries of 'Victoria', which brought an amazing experience to a perfect conclusion.

Chapter Five
ART OF THE COMPOSER

It is hard to know which of the other aspects of Britten the musician would have taken precedence had he not been first and foremost a composer. He certainly could have made a career for himself as a pianist in his own right, and as a conductor he has won world-wide respect

BRITTEN does not compose at the piano. He through-composes, and usually has a precise idea of what he is going to put down on paper before he actually starts. Much as Mozart did, in fact. In this way he works out form and texture in a sharply defined way so that he knows exactly what he wants and how to achieve it. During composition he will revise extensively until the manuscript is sent off to be copied, but then rarely after that. He has, however, come back to works years later and carried out fairly substantial revision. Also, when a work is in rehearsal, if a performer is in difficulties, Britten is prepared to adjust what he has written.

He spends about eight hours a day composing, or it may be twelve when he is scoring. There is, however, no rhythm to the amount he turns out. It may vary enormously. He is a great believer in routine, usually breakfasting at eight and he is at work by nine. He works until about one o'clock, lunches, takes a walk, and returns to work from five until eight p.m. He goes to bed early, but will work late on scoring if he has to, but not so on composition.

He composes mostly at home, and he finds walks by the sea a stimulus. For the same reason, he likes car and train journeys, since they help him to sort out his ideas. He wrote the thirteen-part fugue from *The Turn of the Screw* in the train between Ipswich and London, and for once Imogen Holst found his manuscript that is usually so clear, difficult to transcribe. Although he travels a good deal for recital tours, he rarely composes whilst he is on tour, for Aldeburgh is where his heart is. It is there that he has done virtually all his composing since he came back from America, except for Venice, which is a city he adores, and finds unique. The première of *The Turn of the Screw* was given there, at Teatro la Fenice, and *Curlew River* was written there, as well as a large part of *The Prodigal Son*. If he is prevented from completing a work he becomes very impatient, and if he is obliged to leave Aldeburgh when he is in the middle of composing a work he becomes so fretful that on several occasions he has become ill. His state of mind is reflected in his body, which is probably why he was so ill before he eventually decided to leave America.

Britten has never abandoned tonality in his works. He has used the twelve-note method in *The Turn of the Screw*, for example, but he feels that serialism is somewhat arbitrary in its rules, and is disturbed by its limitations because he can never see it being part of the ordinary music-maker's music-making. As far as he is concerned, then, serialism makes it impossible to write in such a way that will avoid inhibiting amateurs and children.

He has professed on many occasions that he wants to write for people, and bearing in mind his great emphasis on professionalism, the professional must know how to do this. He should therefore be able to write for amateurs just as well as for professionals. He once said in an interview: 'What annoys me . . . is the ineptitude of some professionals who don't know their stuff. I have no patience with that.'

This lack of patience extends not only to composers but to the musicians with whom Britten works. Imogen Holst even used the word 'relentless' to describe him. It is indeed a curious word to use of a person like Britten, but the people who work with him have not only to be good, they have to be very good indeed, and prepared to get better, moreover. It is in this respect that Britten may be said to be relentless, and of course he is with himself, too. There can never be any compromise, because if one is to communicate properly, then only the very best will do. Moreover, Britten finds that the quality of his work is not affected if he is ill, or not particularly keen to work on a given day.

When writing for instruments, Britten's approach has always been to find out the inherent possibilities of each particular instrument, and then exploit them in a way that enriches the literature of that particular instrument permanently.

His own chief instrument is of course the piano, and one of his earliest published works, dating from 1934, is the suite for piano, *Holiday Diary* (Op. 5), which is dedicated to Arthur Benjamin, with whom he studied piano at the Royal College. Britten's *Piano Concerto* in D (Op. 13) followed in 1938, though he revised it in 1945. He gave the first performance of it himself in the old Queen's Hall, London, with the BBC Symphony Orchestra conducted by Sir Henry Wood. He had been a frequent visitor there with Frank Bridge, and they had heard several first performances there together. Britten said himself of the work that it 'was conceived with the idea of exploiting the various important characteristics of the piano, such as its enormous compass, its percussive quality, and its suitability for figuration; so that it is not by any means a symphony with piano, but rather a *bravura* concerto with orchestral accompaniment'. When he revised it in 1945 he

The old Queen's Hall in London, photographed towards the end of the last century. It was here that Britten was soloist with the BBC Symphony Orchestra in the first performance of his piano concerto in 1938. Three years later the hall was destroyed by enemy action

withdrew the third movement and replaced it with a new one. When Aaron Copland visited Britten at Snape in the summer of 1938, Britten had played through to him the concerto which he had just finished. Copland said that he was struck with the obvious 'flair for idiomatic piano writing' but then went on to say that he had some reservations as to the actual 'substance of the musical materials'. There would also seem to be more than a hint in Britten's own description of his aims in the writing of the *Concerto* that he wanted to get away from some of the big Romantic piano concertos – and here a work such as Brahms' Second piano concerto springs to mind – which are more in the nature of symphonies with piano.

A subsequent work for piano and string orchestra, *Young Apollo*, was written for the Canadian Broadcasting Corporation in 1939, and was designated as Op. 16, but the composer subsequently withdrew it.

Britten's next major work for piano and orchestra – *Diversions on a Theme* (Op. 21) – is typical of his ability to exploit some particular aspect of a situation and turn it to advantage. By this time he was in America, and he wrote this work for the left-handed Viennese pianist Paul Wittgenstein. At no time did Britten try to produce anything that would seem like a two-handed approach. On the contrary, he stressed the single-handed approach. He therefore concentrated on trills and scales, arpeggios, agility over the keyboard and repeated notes. Until 1951 Wittgenstein had the sole performing rights of the work, and then in 1954 Britten revised it.

There followed a series of works for two pianos, first of

which was the *Introduction and Rondo alla Burlesca* (Op. 23, No. 1), 1940, and then he went to Escondido, California, the following summer, where he wrote *Mazurka Elegiaca* (Op. 23, No. 2). In Escondido he stayed with the pianist duo Ethel Bartlett and Rae Robertson, who gave the first performance of *Mazurka Elegiaca* in New York Town Hall at the end of 1941. The 'Elegiaca' of the title is appropriate since it is dedicated to the memory of Paderewski. In fact it was intended originally for a memorial volume to Paderewski, but was not included in the end, because Britten made a mistake in writing for two pianos. The commission had specified only one.

When Britten returned to Amityville on Long Island in the autumn of that year he wrote another work for two pianos, *Scottish Ballad* (Op. 26), for two pianos and orchestra, which he dedicated to Ethel Bartlett and Rae Robertson. They gave the first performance of it, with the Cincinatti Symphony Orchestra conducted by Eugène Goossens, in November 1941.

Once Britten returned to England he published nothing more for the piano apart from a *Night Piece* (*Notturno*), which he wrote for the Leeds International Piano Competition in 1963, and the cadenzas for Mozart's E flat major piano concerto (K. 482), which he wrote for a performance of the work by Richter, which Britten conducted, at the Aldeburgh Festival. The operas have naturally absorbed Britten to a large extent, but he has not completely abandoned the piano, since the song cycles for voice and piano continue to appear, and the piano parts are often very difficult, and always pianistic in their approach.

Works for instruments other than the piano have tended to owe their genesis to Britten's response to individuals. His early *Phantasy* (Op. 2), 1932, is a quartet in one movement for oboe, violin, viola and 'cello, and was dedicated to Leon Goossens, who gave the first performance of it. Britten's other work for oboe was written for Joy Boughton, who gave its performance during the Aldeburgh Festival in 1951. It is *Six Metamorphoses after Ovid* (Op. 49), and has become one of the few notable pieces of music written for an unaccompanied wind instrument in this century.

The previous year the festival had seen the première of *Lachrymae* (Op. 48), which are described as 'reflections' on a song by John Dowland, and are for viola and piano. The work is dedicated to William Primrose, who also gave the first performance of it with Britten at the piano. Britten had learnt the viola as a child, and it was through his teacher, Audrey Alston, that he first met Frank Bridge. Britten dedicated his *Simple Symphony* (Op. 4) to her. Boyd Neel recalled that when his orchestra had its first run-through of the *Variations on a Theme of Frank Bridge* (Op. 10), which the orchestra played for the first time at the Salzburg Festival in 1937, both Britten and Bridge attended. The solo viola player had some difficulty with the harmonics in a passage in the *Wiener Walzer* variation. Harmonics are obtained on a stringed instrument by stopping the string as if to play an ordinary note, and then touching the string again at a point between where it has been stopped and the bridge, so that when it is bowed a very much higher note is produced. It requires a skilled player to produce these notes, therefore, especially when he is playing a fairly fast moving passage. At the rehearsal both Britten and Bridge picked up the viola in turn and played the passage without a mistake. Now Britten's feats on the viola tend to be restricted to playing the one note in Purcell's *Fantasia upon one Note*, but he has never lost his ability to write for the instrument as 'gratefully' as he writes for voices.

The talent of the horn player Dennis Brain was combined with the vocal talent of Peter Pears for the *Serenade* (Op. 31) for tenor, horn and strings in 1943, and *Canticle Three* (Still falls the Rain – The Raids, 1940, Night and Dawn). It was written in 1954 and had its first performance the following January, again with Brain and Pears, and Britten at the piano. Britten used the horn subsequently as one of the obbligato instruments in his *Nocturne* (Op. 60), 1958, for tenor voice, seven obbligato instruments and string orchestra.

Britten has not forgotten the more humble members of the wind family, either. In 1955 he wrote an *Alpine Suite* for recorder trio to divert his artist friend Mary Potter who had injured her leg whilst skiing. The movements are pure programme music – 'Arrival at Zermatt; Swiss Clock; Nursery Slopes; Alpine Scene; Moto perpetuo: Down the Piste; Farewell to Zermatt.' Then there is the *Scherzo*, dating from the same year, for recorder quartet, which is dedicated to the Aldeburgh Music Club. One might also add here the Morris Dance from his opera *Gloriana*, which has been arranged for two descant recorders.

Britten's writing for strings began with an unpublished *Phantasy* for string quartet, 1932, and *Alla Quartetto Serioso*, 1933, three movements of an uncompleted string quartet with the title 'Go play, boy, play.' During the winter of 1933–4,

Opposite: Benjamin Britten and Peter Pears at the Maltings, Snape. The artistic partnership they established before World War II has now lasted over thirty-five years, and has produced an unbroken stream of compositions and memorable performances

Overleaf: The windmill at Drinkstone, Suffolk, in a landscape typical of Britten's native county, and the countryside in which he so often walks for relaxation and inspiration

however, he produced one of his string works which he felt worthy of publication, and that was the *Simple Symphony* (Op. 4), which may be played either by string orchestra or string quartet. The score says that it is 'entirely based on material from works which the composer wrote between the ages of nine and twelve. Although the development of these themes is in many places quite new, there are large stretches of the work which are taken bodily from the early pieces, save for the re-scoring for strings.'

Probably the symphony's main interest, in the context of Britten's subsequent career, is in the fact that it showed at an early stage that he had a tendency to write for groups of instruments rather than large-scale works for the entire orchestra. The *Variations on a Theme of Frank Bridge*, 1937, were to confirm this, and had an amazing success. The Boyd Neel orchestra gave the first performance, and it was for that orchestra's tenth birthday that Britten wrote his *Prelude and Fugue* (Op. 29), 1943. It is for 18-part string orchestra, with 10 violins, 3 violas, 3 'cellos and 2 double-basses. In an article in *Tempo* of February 1944 he said: 'I am attracted by the many features of the strings. For instance the possibilities of elaborate *divisi* — the effect of many voices of the same kind. There is also the infinite variety of colour — the use of mutes, pizzicato, harmonics and so forth. Then again, there is the great dexterity in technique of string players. Generally speaking, I like to think of the smaller combinations of players, and I deplore the tendency of present-day audiences to expect only the luscious 'tutti' effect from an orchestra.'

The violin as a solo instrument has not inspired very much music from Britten. It may well have been more of an inspiration to him had he met a particular performer with whom he reached a close understanding, as for example with Rostropovich and the 'cello. There is, however, the *Suite* (Op. 6) for violin and piano, written in the months between November 1934 and June 1935, and the *Violin Concerto* (Op. 15), written in Canada in 1939 and then revised in 1958. Antonio Brosa gave the first performances of both works; the *Suite* in April 1936 at the ISCM Festival in Barcelona that year, with Britten at the piano (though three of the movements had been performed previously in London in 1934); and the *Concerto* in March 1940 in New York with the New York Philharmonic Orchestra and John Barbirolli conducting. Brosa edited the violin part of the concerto.

The work demands great technical ability from the soloist, and shows once again Britten's habit of exploiting the features of an instrument to the full. The last movement is a passacaglia, which is the first time that Britten used the device, which he subsequently has favoured so much.

Britten was once asked by an interviewer whether the whip was not his favourite instrument, since he seemed to include it frequently in his scoring. With apparent total seriousness, Britten replied that he thought not. What he prefers is the wealth of sounds that are inherent in many instruments, but which so often have been ignored, particularly in the great wave of sounds that issue from the symphony orchestra as handled during the Romantic and immediately post-Romantic era. Conversely, one of the most disturbing tendencies in the greater part of contemporary music is the fact that instruments are not exploited subtly, in a way that capitalises on their unique personalities, but they are simply used to produce sounds of any sort.

One might, from a study of the instrumentation of Britten's works, deduce that he had a slight preference for the alto saxophone. He used it in *Our Hunting Fathers*, *Mont Juic* (with an ad lib. tenor saxophone), and as an ad lib. in both *Sinfonia da Requiem* and *Diversions* for (left-hand) piano and orchestra. It reappeared in *Billy Budd*, and again in *The Prince of the Pagodas*. As one might expect, the viola is another instrument that Britten has brought more into the limelight. Furthermost, the alto flute was given a part in both *The Rape of Lucretia* and *Albert Herring* — since they were both written for the same ensemble — and a bass flute was brought into *The Turn of the Screw*.

One of Britten's most genial touches of orchestral colour occurred quite by chance. Whilst he was writing *Noye's Fludde* he was visited by some members of the Aldeburgh Youth Club who had come to choose from the foreign stamps that arrive by almost every post at the Red House. The boys told him that they had a handbell practice that evening, so Britten asked them to come and play to him. He was so delighted with the sound they produced that he wrote them a part into the score of *Noye's Fludde* at the crucial moment when the rainbow appears and God promises that there will be no more wrath and vengeance.

Naturally this is not to say that Britten was never attracted to writing for the full orchestra. His Opus 1 is the *Sinfonietta*,

Opposite above: Britten conducting during the filming of his television opera *Owen Wingrave*. Despite the fact that he is not particularly addicted to television, he saw the commission as an interesting challenge, and set about it with his usual practical approach

Opposite below: A rehearsal taking place on the set of *Owen Wingrave*, Act I, the family seat Paramore. The intimacy of the television presentation gave Britten a new kind of freedom in his handling of his material, and one which subsequently adapted relatively easily to the opera house stage

for ten instruments or basically a chamber orchestra, and the *Mont Juic Suite* of Catalan dances (written with Lennox Berkeley), 1937, uses the basic orchestra with the addition of harp, and saxophones if desired. He was therefore making moves in the direction of the full orchestra, but as he himself has said: 'Of course with such a wonderful and sensitive instrument as the modern symphony orchestra to hand, one wants to write for it. But my inclination is not to use all of it all the time. I like to use contrasting sections; and there are many occasions when far smaller units – forms of chamber orchestra – seem nearer to one's ideas.' Britten went on to acknowledge the part played by Stravinsky and Schoenberg in paving the way in this respect. It is also easy to see why Britten finds the orchestral sounds of Beethoven and Brahms so unsatisfactory. The ear is overwhelmed with sheer sound – and even in some of the piano music, too. Britten is searching for clarity, for textural clarity, for clarity of expression. For perfect clarity. 'Music for me is clarification; I try to clarify, to refine, to sensitise... My technique is to tear all waste away; to achieve perfect clarity of expression, that is my aim.'

It is perhaps surprising, therefore, that Britten has written only two string quartets – No. 1 in D (Op. 25), 1941, and No. 2 in C (Op. 36), 1945. The first was dedicated to the great American patroness of the arts Mrs Elizabeth Sprague Coolidge, who commissioned it. The second was written to commemorate the 250th anniversary of the death of Purcell. It may be that Britten will return to the form in the future, or it may be that he feels he cannot use the medium to say what he has to say – or rather that he can say it better in another medium. As one might expect, the second quartet has some Purcellian elements in it, particularly the use of a chacony as the third movement.

About the time that Britten wrote the first quartet he was also working on the orchestration of *Matinées Musicales* (Op. 24), 1941, which was a second suite of five movements from Rossini's music for orchestra. Britten wrote this at the request of the director of the American Ballet Company, Lincoln Kirstein (to whom it is dedicated), so as to form a ballet along with *Soirées Musicales* (Op. 9) which was also a suite of five movements from Rossini that Britten had arranged in 1936. Balanchine did the choreography, for the American Ballet Company, and the ballet was produced in 1941. Britten had previously used Rossini's music in the documentary *Men of the Alps*, 1936, and in a silhouette film *The Tocher*, devised and produced by Lotte Reiniger for the GPO Film Unit in 1938.

In 1940 Britten orchestrated Chopin's *Les Sylphides* for the New York Ballet Theatre, but he has written only one ballet of his own, *The Prince of the Pagodas* (Op. 57), 1956. Several of his works, however, have been used for ballets from time to time. *The Prince of the Pagodas* was not a lasting success, and in the context of Britten's career is of more significance from the point of view of the orchestration and its interest in Balinese music.

Britten first became interested in Balinese music – or made some acquaintance with it – whilst he was in America in 1941. He met Colin McPhee and the two of them recorded some Balinese music that McPhee had transcribed for two pianos. Some thirteen or fourteen years later, when Britten was thinking about writing a full-length ballet in conjunction with John Cranko, the idea of introducing an Oriental element came back to him.

At the end of 1955 and in early 1956 Britten and Pears were on a tour during which they visited Bali, Japan and India. In Bali, Britten was very taken with the richness of the music, from the point of view of melody, rhythm, orchestral texture and form. Then the way in which the *gamelan* orchestra works – each instrument plays a version of a short tune of five notes but comes in at a different place in a different tempo – influenced the concept of the parables for church performance, where there is no conductor, and phrases in the accompanying instruments may be repeated until instruments and singers reach the same fixed point. The idea of the theme of the first parable came more specifically from Japan, though on the same tour.

When it came to the writing of the score of *The Prince of the Pagodas*, at least in the second act scene with the pagodas, Britten brought into the score a vibraphone, celesta, piano, xylophone, bells, tomtoms and gongs. This was one of the very rare occasions when Britten was behind with his work, in this case with the scoring, and so the first performance had to be put back from September 1956 to January 1957.

It was perhaps unfortunate that a fairy-tale had been chosen as the subject-matter for the ballet, since one tends to think of most ballet as being concerned with fairy-tales – certainly the classical ballets. Moreover, Cranko had said that he did not want a pastiche of the classical ballet style, but an opportunity for some creative choreography. In the circumstances, then, it

Although several of his works have been choreographed, Britten has only written one ballet, *The Prince of the Pagodas*. It was first presented at Covent Garden in 1957, choreographed by John Cranko

Richard Morris in *The Prince of the Pagodas*, which has not been revived since 1957, despite being seen in London, New York and Milan that year. The score calls for some of Britten's most colourful and exotic sound effects, and was influenced by music he had heard in the Far East

seems odd to have chosen the particular theme of *The Prince of the Pagodas*, which is essentially a fairy-tale. Cranko felt that this did not matter. It could be left to the audience to make of it what they would, as far as the plot was concerned. But as far as Cranko was concerned, it would be the various images that would provide the creative element in the choreography.

Unfortunately the fairy-tale element seemed to eclipse this aspect, and the ballet has not won a permanent place in the repertoire. This is a pity, since the music may be condemned to obscurity. The *Pas de Six* from the ballet was performed separately in 1957 by the City of Birmingham Symphony Orchestra, however, and the music may yet find its way into the orchestral repertoire.

Communication for Britten is, in his music, of paramount importance. He has said that if he did not communicate he would consider that he had failed. This will be a matter ultimately for the future to decide, but from what he has written already, and the response to his music, he would seem to have communicated to a great many people.

When U Thant spoke in the United Nations on 24 October 1965, he said: 'Today he (Britten) speaks for all of us, with an eloquence we lack, in a medium of which he is master.' This was no small tribute to be paid to any human being, as indeed was the very fact that Britten had been commissioned to write a work to celebrate the twentieth anniversary of the United Nations in the first place. The anthem that he wrote for that occasion, *Voices for Today*, was given a simultaneous première in New York, Paris and London.

Some critics have implied that Britten has been too much swayed, in the process of communicating, by considerations of what people would like to hear rather than telling them what he wanted to tell them. This seems almost presumptuous, and denotes a failure on their part to evaluate properly what he has done. It would also seem to be influenced by a very common view that good art must be virtually unintelligible.

Pastiche is another charge that has been levelled at Britten's music by some critics. Pastiche implies a deliberate attempt to pass off music as being the style, or even the music itself, of another person or country. Britten has never done this except for a deliberate effect, as in the opera within an opera in *A Midsummer Night's Dream*. There he had to find a convention that would point up the contrast between the sophisticated Court of Athens and the Rustics, between his own music in the

Below: Children have always had a special place in Britten's music, and he has done an immense amount to ensure that they hear and play music written with them in mind. Here he signs autographs in Budapest

Below right: Foreign trips are hard work for Britten and Pears, both on and off the concert platform. There have been holidays abroad, but moments such as this visit to Tivoli Gardens in Copenhagen in 1952 are rare

Opposite above: A portrait of Britten in his fiftieth year in his study at Aldeburgh. It is here that most of his music has been composed over the last fifteen years or so, with only occasional inspiration from elsewhere

Opposite below: The composer takes a dip in the sea at Aldeburgh in 1952, a year of extensive foreign travel and concentrated work on the coronation opera *Gloriana*

opera and the sort of music the Rustics might sing in relation to it. He came up with the brilliant and highly entertaining solution of a parody of 19th-century opera.

He came near to pastiche – but for a very special reason – in *The Prince of the Pagodas*, and again in *Gloriana* in the Earl of Essex's lute song. The music he wrote for that song owes a great deal to real Elizabethan music, and although he has written a beautiful piece of music, it is not quite far enough away, relatively, from the setting of the opera. He was more successful in *A Midsummer Night's Dream* in this respect.

In *Curlew River* the music may have an Oriental feel, and some of the instrumental technique involved may draw its inspiration from Oriental techniques, but the intent is never simply to produce something that might sound like Japanese music. In fact at the very heart of the music is the plainsong hymn *Te lucis ante terminum*, which could hardly be more rooted in Western culture. To have produced simply a pastiche of Japanese music or, on the other hand, to have attempted a pseudo-medieval musical drama would both have been as bad as each other. As it is, Britten has, with his usual flair, penetrated to the inherent possibilities of the two elements, of the two cultures even, and produced something which is not simply a hybrid, but a new form of musical art.

But what must surely impress even the severest critic of Britten's music in its overall aspect, is the sheer professionalism of his writing for individual instruments. He regards it as part of his job as a composer, but if more composers could write for instruments with half his flair, the outlook for music would be considerably more bright than it is at the present time.

Chapter Six
BRITTEN'S PHILOSOPHY

Britten in the Berlin Opera House for the performance of his *War Requiem*, given there on 18 November 1962, and conducted by Colin Davis. The crosses in the background symbolise the German organisation for war graves

MUCH of Britten's philosophy is set out in the speech he made when he received the first Aspen Award in 1964. The award was established by Robert O. Anderson of Roswell, New Mexico, chairman of the Institute of Humanistic Studies at Aspen, Colorado, USA. The citation ran as follows: 'To Benjamin Britten, who, as a brilliant composer, performer, and interpreter through music of human feelings, moods, and thoughts, has truly inspired man to understand, clarify and appreciate more fully his own nature, purpose and destiny.' Citations are almost always grandiose, and at times words can be a positive disincentive to comprehension. Britten's reply helps to focus the mind once more.

'I certainly write music for human beings – directly and deliberately. I consider their voices, the range, the power, the subtlety, and the colour potentialities of them. I consider the instruments they play – their most expressive and suitable individual sonorities, and where I may be said to have invented an instrument (such as the Slung Mugs of *Noye's Fludde*) I have borne in mind the pleasure the young performers will have in playing it. I also take note of the *human* circumstances of music, of its environment and conventions; for instance, I try to write dramatically effective music for the theatre . . . And then the best music to listen to in a great Gothic church is the polyphony which was written for it, and was calculated for its resonance: this was my approach in the *War Requiem* . . . I believe, you see, in *occasional music* . . . almost every piece I have ever written has been composed with a certain occasion in mind, and usually for definite performers, and certainly always *human* ones.'

This does not mean, however, that Britten consciously limits himself to the occasion, or even to the performers. One tends to think of much of the vocal music for high voice, for example, as being sung by Peter Pears, but his is not the only voice capable of singing it. Indeed, one of Britten's most successful vocal works, *Les Illuminations*, was written for the soprano Sophie Wyss, who had given the first performance of *Our Hunting Fathers*.

Britten pays so much attention to the circumstances in which his work is to be performed because he wants the performers to enjoy it, and because he is more likely to get his message across by means of music that people enjoy or can enter into the spirit of, than by imposing his artistic vision on them willy nilly. This does not mean that he will accept every commission, or that he compromises his artistic integrity. He explained in the same speech at Aspen that he had refused on several occasions to write a work as a memorial to J. F. Kennedy, not because he felt no sympathy with the idea, but because he had been so moved by the event of his assassination when it happened, that the time was not yet ripe for him to be able to do so. Nor are the conditions imposed by a particular occasion simply a restriction for Britten. He constantly refers back to them during the process of composition, and they become a challenge and an inspiration.

'When I am asked to compose a work for an occasion, great or small, I want to know in some detail the conditions of the place where it will be performed, the size and acoustics, what instruments or singers will be available and suitable, the kind of people who will hear it, and what language they will understand – and even sometimes the age of the listeners and performers. For it is futile to offer children music by which they are bored, or which makes them feel inadequate or frustrated, which may set them against music for ever; and it is insulting to address anyone in a language which they do not understand.'

To get some idea of the incredible scope of Britten's occasional music, examples are found throughout his career. They vary enormously in concept and the sort of occasion for which they were written. *The Ballad of Little Musgrave and Lady Barnard* for male voices and piano, 1943, was written for British prisoners-of-war in a camp in Germany and posted out to them in sections. The *Five Flower Songs* (Op. 47), 1950, for unaccompanied mixed chorus, were written for the silver wedding anniversary of Leonard and Dorothy Elmhirst of Dartington Hall. In 1958 Britten wrote an eight-part canon for voices and piano to celebrate the 60th birthday of Martin Hürlimann – who commissioned the first book ever on Britten, in German – and in 1959 and 1960 respectively, two fanfares, the first for the Magna Carta pageant at Bury St Edmunds, and the second for the launching of *SS Oriana*. Even to the writing of a fanfare Britten brings his expertise, and for the Magna Carta pageant scored for trumpets in different keys because they were to be at a distance from each other.

Cantata Academica (Op. 62) was written for the quincentenary of Basle University in 1959, and *Cantata Misericordium* (Op. 69) in 1963 for the centenary of the Red Cross. *Voices for Today* (Op. 75) was an anthem for the twentieth anniversary of the United Nations, whereas the overture for chorus and

Abraham prepares to sacrifice Isaac, from the Fitzroy tomb in Framlingham Parish Church. This theme was the subject of Britten's Canticle II, and reappears in the *War Requiem*, where Britten quotes from his own music

orchestra *The Building of the House* (Op. 79) was for a more domestic occasion, namely the opening of the new concert hall, the converted Maltings at Snape.

Music that is equally occasional, though in a very different way, is the *War Requiem*, written for the consecration of the new cathedral at Coventry. But of course it is more than this, it is the symbol of the healing of the wounds caused by World War II – and even World War I for that matter – and of the rift in the relationship between Britain and Germany. But far beyond that, to Britten as a confirmed pacifist, it is an opportunity to pronounce his views to the world. On the title page of the *War Requiem* he put some phrases from Owen's unpublished preface to his poems. 'My subject is war, and the pity of War. The Poetry is in the pity . . . All a poet can do today is warn.' Owen had long been one of Britten's preferred poets, and for the *War Requiem* he had the idea of taking the Latin text of the Mass for the Dead, and interpolating, or juxtaposing, a selection of Owen's poems. The words of the Mass are accordingly set in a more or less conventional way for chorus and orchestra, and the poems are scored for soloists and a chamber orchestra of twelve. Since the two soloists are in fact tenor and bass (dictated by the last poem, *Strange Meeting*, in which a British soldier meets a German soldier he had killed), then it seemed better, for purposes of contrast, to have a soprano soloist with the main choir, to which was added a boys' choir.

When Britten took Owen's poem *The Parable of the Old Men and the Young*, which is the Abraham and Isaac story in modern terms, Britten made a deliberate musical reference to *Canticle Two*, his own treatment of the Abraham and Isaac story as found in the Chester Miracle Plays. The reference to Abraham in the *War Requiem* springs in the first place, of course, from the Latin text of the Offertory in the Mass, which reads in translation '. . . which he promised to Abraham and his seed . . .' Britten then takes it up, via his own music, to Owen's poem:

> *When lo! an angel called him out of heaven,*
> *Saying, Lay not thy hand upon the lad,*
> . . . .
> *Offer the Ram of Pride instead of him.*
> *But the old man would not so, but slew his son, –*
> *And half the seed of Europe, one by one.*

SS *Orland* was launched on 3 November 1960, and Britten wrote a fanfare for the occasion, thus carrying into practice his belief that composers should be integral members of the community and serve it with occasional music

Another highly occasional composition was Britten's fanfare for the St Edmundsbury Magna Carta pageant in 1959. On this occasion he brought his very practical and professional mind to bear, and realised that if the trumpets were to be placed apart, tuning would present a problem. He therefore wrote in different keys for them

Britten conducted his *War Requiem* in Germany in the baroque splendour of Ottobeuren basilica with Peter Pears as tenor soloist and Dietrich Fischer-Dieskau as baritone soloist

One sees here Britten's mind at work linking up the various strands across the centuries, a thing at which he has excelled all his life.

The *War Requiem* won immediate acceptance. The recording sold a huge number of copies almost as soon as it was released, and people have been known to wear out sets of the records through playing them so frequently.

To describe Britten's music as occasional, therefore, is by no means an insult, especially when one appreciates his own conception of the term. He wants music to be even more occasional, in the sense that he regrets the fact that today it is so easy for people to switch on a radio or tape recorder, or put on a gramophone record, and have music instantly. He would like people to prepare more for listening to a piece of music, to make it more of an occasion – in fact – than it often is. Just as the musicians have to rehearse, practise and learn their notes, so Britten wants the listener to work at home learning something about the composer whose music he is to hear, and the particular work that is to be performed. Even saving up to buy the ticket and making a journey to the concert hall help, in Britten's estimation, to make more of an occasion of a performance. In his own words: '... a musical experience needs three human beings at least. It requires a composer, a performer, and a listener; and unless these three take part together there is no musical experience...'

For Britten this 'holy triangle' – as he calls it – needs to exist not only in the actual performance, but in society at large, certainly as far as the musician has a place in that society. If society – or the State – accepted composers, and all artists and musicians for that matter, as integral members of that society, then there would be a two-way exchange. The State would make life possible for the artist or musician, and in return there could be special music for football matches, receptions, elections, and presentations of awards. After all, what is today some of Handel's most popular music was written for very official occasions. This may seem a rather Utopian viewpoint, but Britten knows and believes that 'finding one's place in society as a composer is not a straightforward job'. For one thing, Britten has often lamented the philistinism of this country. On the other hand, he has also said: 'I am touched deeply by the response given me.'

Of course the relationship between the artist and society is always a difficult one. If the State – or society – were to accept musicians as an integral part of it, then it would seem logical for the State to require the fulfilment of at least some conditions. In matters of ideology this could be very difficult, and Britten is aware of this. He has seen, more than most people from the West, what life is like for the artist behind the Iron Curtain. But Britten has said quite positively '... it is the composer's duty, as a member of society, to speak to or for his fellow human beings'. 'Duty' is a strong word, but in Britten's philosophy it goes back to his very early days with Frank Bridge. It was Bridge's tuition that made Britten so professional in his outlook – so professional at times that he is highly critical of those composers who are not, in his estimation, professional.

For his personal taste, his favourite composers are Bach, Mozart, Schubert, Verdi, Tchaikovsky, Mahler, Berg – and of course, Purcell. Britten's concern for Purcell's music amounts

at times to a personal crusade. He staggered a critic who once asked him from whom he had learned to set English poetry to music, when he answered 'Purcell'. His *Canticle One* (Op. 40), for high voice and piano, to Francis Quarles' poem *A Divine Rapture*, was consciously modelled on Purcell's Divine Hymns, though Britten maintained that at the time – 1947 – few people realised the fact.

What Britten learned from Purcell about setting words to music is summed up in what he himself wrote in the Sadler's Wells Opera Book (No. 3) on *Peter Grimes*: 'Good recitative should transform the natural intonations and rhythms of everyday speech into memorable musical phrases (as with Purcell)...' A vivid illustration of this in operation comes from Britten's *A Midsummer Night's Dream*, towards the end, where Oberon calls for music. Britten sets the first syllable of the word 'music' to a single four-note descending phrase, which in the counter-tenor voice (for which it is written) is in the centre of the register, and therefore beautifully placed vocally. In addition, the rich vowel gives the singer the opportunity to project the voice.

One realises exactly how gifted Britten is in this respect when one compares the translation of, for example, *A Midsummer Night's Dream* into French. In the first concert performance in French given in the Maison de la Radio in Paris, and then subsequently broadcast, the translator of the text seemed entirely unaware of what Britten had done, and wrote a string of syllables – one to every note of the phrase – in a clumsy succession of consonants and sharp vowels. Britten also, incidentally, retained the spelling 'Tytania' which is in the Quarto edition of Shakespeare's play, and gives a longer, richer sound to the first syllable of the name than 'Titania' would do.

But beyond the question of setting words, Britten has deep

Opposite left: Edith Sitwell (1884–1964), photographed in 1956. Britten set her poem *Still Falls the Rain*, and she dedicated her poem *Praise We Great Men*, to him, and read it in the Purcell celebrations in 1959

Opposite centre: Britten's concern for the music of Henry Purcell has been something of a personal crusade, and there is no doubt that he has been deeply influenced by that composer's music

Opposite right: Gustav Mahler (1860–1911) has always been one of Britten's favourite composers, and he admired his musical form from student days. It was appropriate, therefore, that Britten's *Nocturne* should be dedicated to Mahler's widow

insight into Purcell the man, and his music. He contributed a very practical essay – 'On realising the Continuo in Purcell's songs' – to the volume published in 1959, *Henry Purcell 1659–1695* (edited by Imogen Holst). His essay ends: 'I know there are many other ways of realising Purcell's figured basses... I hope there will be many more, and done with plenty of boldness of imagination, for what has kept so many of these wonderful treasures locked up in obscurity has been creative dullness or too much reverence. Purcell would have hated these two qualities above all; at least, that is the feeling one has after getting to know him through even these few works.'

Britten has written his *Holy Sonnets of John Donne* (Op. 35), for high voice and piano, and his *String Quartet* No. 2 in C (Op. 36) as an act of homage to Purcell on the 250th anniversary of his death, which fell on 21 November 1945. Soon after this occasion he decided to work with Peter Pears on a performing edition of Purcell's works. Publication began the following year, and included secular songs and duets from *Orpheus Britannicus*, and religious and vocal music from *Harmonia Sacra*. In addition there has been *The Queen's Epicedium* (Purcell's elegy on the death of Queen Mary), 1695; the *Golden Sonata* for two violins, 'cello and piano; and the *Chacony* in G minor for string orchestra. Anyone who has seen Britten rehearse this last work will realise how much he cares about Purcell's music, and how thoroughly he understands it. A performing edition of *Dido and Aeneas* (1689), was also envisaged, and was actually advertised in the Glyndebourne programme of 1946 for the next year, but it did not take place until 1951. Britten regards this opera as a masterpiece, but laments the fact that it is only rarely performed because it is not a box-office success.

Another occasion for the increasing of the public's knowledge and awareness of Purcell's music was provided by the tercentenary of his birth in 1959. In addition to the volume mentioned above, Britten contributed a performance, which he conducted, of Purcell's *Ode for St Cecilia*, at the Royal Festival Hall, London. Dame Edith Sitwell wrote a poem for the occasion, *Praise We Great Men*, which she dedicated to Britten and read that evening from the platform. As an integral part of the occasion it hardly succeeded, but the words remain, and the fact that Dame Edith went to read them, gave the occasion added significance.

In some ways Britten's position when he decided to write *Peter Grimes* was similar to that of Purcell when he wrote his preface to *Dioclesian* in 1691. 'Poetry and Painting have arriv'd to their perfection in our own Country; Musick is yet but in its Nonage, a forward Child which gives hope of what it may be hereafter in England, when the Masters of it shall find more Encouragement.' By that Purcell did not mean simply moral encouragement. He meant financial encouragement, which has been, and presumably always will be, the cry of composers over the centuries. ''Tis now learning Italian, which is its best Master, and studying a little of the French Air, to give it somewhat more of Gayety and Fashion.' There is a remarkable parallel here to the fact that Britten chose to set French words for *Les Illuminations*, and Italian words for the *Seven Sonnets of Michelangelo*. 'Thus being further from the Sun, we are of later Growth than our Neighbour Countries, and must be content to shake off our Barbarity by degrees. The present Age seems already dispos'd to be refin'd, and to distinguish betwixt wild Fancy, and a just, numerous Composition.' Britten's condemnation of the basic philistinism of this country does not need repeating.

Of course here Purcell had been thinking of music specifically in relation to the setting of words, as the passage immediately preceding the one just quoted shows: 'Music and Poetry have ever been acknowledged Sisters, which walking hand in hand supports the other; As Poetry is the harmony of Words, So Musick is that of Notes: and as Poetry is a Rise above Prose and Oratory, so is Musick the exaltation of Poetry. Both of them may excel apart, but sure they are most excellent when they are joyn'd because nothing is then wanting to either of their Perfections; for thus they appear like Wit and Beauty in the same Person.'

It is obviously no mere coincidence that Michael Tippett, as his contribution to the Purcell tercentenary volume, should write an essay entitled 'Our Sense of Continuity in English Drama and Music,' in which he stressed the crucial importance of Purcell's setting of English words for English composers. He wrote: 'For, more than anyone else, the creative artist needs a sense of continuity.' But he went on to point out that although Purcell's significance is helpful in the writing of opera, Purcell cannot simply be equated with opera. He only wrote one opera, strictly speaking, so it is – according to Tippett – for the setting of words, and musical technique for the theatre, that Purcell is above all important. Tippett went on in the same essay,

The first performance of the *War Requiem* was in Coventry Cathedral in 1962. Heather Harper was the soprano, with Peter Pears and Dietrich Fischer-Dieskau. Britten shared the conducting with Meredith Davies

incidentally, to suggest that for a sense of continuity in English opera, English composers ought to seek a deeper insight into Shakespeare's verse drama, from which to obtain what he calls the 'double pattern of drama and music' which is generally missing from Purcell, although Purcell was looking for it himself.

Of course the attitude of people towards Shakespeare in Purcell's day was very different, and Purcell would have been an even more extraordinary person than he was if he had been able to see Shakespeare in the way that we today are accustomed to see him. But in the light of Tippett's remarks it is interesting that Britten was subsequently to turn *A Midsummer Night's Dream* into an opera in 1960. Tippett concludes: '... if it is really possible that the English composer can see how to use Shakespeare as the master for certain things that are usually only sought for in great operatic composers as such, then our sense of musical continuity with Purcell may be further developed and fructified.'

Had Purcell lived, he might have brought English opera fully into being. As it was, he certainly laid solid foundations for it at the time. With *Peter Grimes*, Britten stood in somewhat the same position. English opera had never got off the ground. In 1779 Dr Johnson condemned Italian opera as 'an exotick and irrational entertainment, which has been always combated, and always has prevailed.' English opera was swamped by foreign opera to the extent that virtually no English composer achieved any very great fame for almost two hundred years, and English people were thought incapable of becoming opera singers – a misconception that lasted even longer. The sense of continuity had been lost. Britten was aware of the fact, and aware no doubt that with *Peter Grimes* he had a chance to establish once more that continuity. In an interview given shortly after he had begun composing the opera, at the beginning of 1944, Britten said: 'I am passionately interested in seeing a successful permanent national opera in existence...'

In a way Britten further strengthened the continuity, and at the same time drew closer together the threads that Michael Tippett described in his essay, when he produced his performing edition of Purcell's *The Fairy Queen* (1692), which was a rearrangement of *A Midsummer Night's Dream*. Britten, Pears and Imogen Holst worked together on a new concert version in 1967, and it was given during the Aldeburgh Festival that year, which also saw a revival of Britten's own *A Midsummer*

Britten's opera to Shakespeare's play *A Midsummer Night's Dream* was presented at Aldeburgh for the first time in 1960, in the enlarged Jubilee Hall. This gave Britten scope for a larger orchestra than hitherto, and the entire work was written in seven months. He had always been very fond of the play, and he and Peter Pears prepared the libretto together. This involved cutting the play by half, but only one line of Shakespeare's text was altered

Night's Dream. Perhaps Purcell's significance for Britten is best summed up in Britten's own words that preface his realisations of Purcell's music: '...it has been the constant endeavour of the arranger to apply to these realisations something of that mixture of clarity, brilliance, tenderness and strangeness which shines out in all Purcell's music'.

Purcell is not the only composer whose works Britten has realised. Consistent with his concern for English opera, in 1948 he decided to make a new performing version of John Gay's ballad opera of 1728, *The Beggar's Opera* (Britten's Op. 43). In Gay's original opera fifty-one out of sixty-nine airs were anonymous, popular tunes, and Britten wanted to keep all of them, for he regarded them as some of the finest national songs, pointing out their close resemblance to Handel and Purcell. In preparing a new version, which he never pretended would be the definitive one, Britten was concerned to do away with the attempts of previous performing editions to present the tunes as simply lyrical and sweet, which had often seriously distorted the original lines, but he subtly used the orchestra to emphasise the peculiar modes in which some of the tunes are written, and the often unusual intervals they contain.

Turning from one kind of lyricism to another, in 1958 Britten made an arrangement of the second movement from Mahler's Third Symphony for reduced orchestra, under the title 'What the Wild Flowers Tell Me'. The *Nocturne* (Op. 60), for tenor, seven obbligato instruments and string orchestra, was dedicated to Mahler's widow, Alma.

It would be wrong to place too much emphasis on one particular point of similarity between two composers and then deduce much from it. However, apart from the very obvious feeling for melodic line and lyricism that both Mahler and Britten have, there is one particular effect, the switching of a chord from major to minor and vice versa, which they both use on occasion to great effect. Mahler used it, for instance, in No. 4 of his *Lieder eines Farhenden Gesellen* ('*Die zwei blauen Augen*') and Britten in his piano accompaniment to the Somerset folksong *O Waly, Waly*. The words of the last verse run:

> O, love is handsome and love is fine,
> and love's a jewel while it is new,
> But when it is old, it groweth cold,
> and fades away like morning dew.

Britten confines the piano part in this last stanza to what one would usually regard as the left-hand part of the accompaniment; in other words there is no note above middle C played by either hand. Already, therefore, one has a very rich and sombre sound in the background. The tonality is basically G major, but for the second half of the stanza Britten slips in an F natural, and on the word 'cold' – which he marks *ppp* in both voice and piano – he moves down to an E flat, which is the minor third of the chord, with a spine-chilling effect, especially if the singer is Peter Pears and the accompanist Britten himself.

Britten and Pears may include a group of these folk songs at the end of a recital, and at one particular recital there was the usual call for an encore. There was a moment's debate between the two performers, and they launched into *The Little Ploughboy*, which was delivered with great accomplishment, but when it came to the second encore, *O Waly, Waly*, which seemed to have been Britten's preference, the audience knew that they had been given a very special musical bonus, and asked for no more. The moment of silence at the end of the song was eloquent in itself.

Whether it is performing as accompanist to Peter Pears or, more recently, conducting for recording purposes Elgar's *Dream of Gerontius* with Pears singing the tenor part, Britten brings to all music his insight and unfailing instinct. When one hears Britten playing a Schubert accompaniment and then looks at the printed page, it seems incredible that what he has just played should be there in black and white, but Britten feels it instinctively, without introducing any extraneous elements whatsoever, and he truly makes the music speak.

Then again, Elgar is not a composer that one normally would associate with Britten, but his reading of the score is sympathetic and, above all, faithful to the composer's intentions, as indeed Britten would like performances of his own music to be.

But in the final analysis, it is for people, and not other musicians, that Britten makes his music, and for him contact with people, with the audience is vital. This does not prevent him from presenting them with what he knows is the best possible performance and the best possible music performed in the best possible way, but without an audience the composer is in danger of getting lost in his ivory tower, and, in Britten's estimation, of no longer speaking in a language that they will understand.

Chapter Seven
CONCLUSION

Britten has conducted many of his own works, but only a selection of those of other composers. Bach and Purcell probably head the list, though more recently Elgar has been added to it

WHEN Britten celebrated his fiftieth birthday in 1963 a volume of essays and contributions from friends and colleagues was published as a tribute to him. It is a curious volume in many ways because it contains an extraordinary mixture of things. But then Britten's range of interests, and the range of his friends, is extraordinarily wide. There are reminiscences, as befits a birthday volume; there are technical contributions about musical matters, as befits a very professional composer; but there are also purely literary contributions from such people as E. M. Forster and Dame Edith Sitwell, and articles on such varied topics as Greek Shadow Theatre and the flora of the Suffolk countryside. That volume represented a distillation of the past, a concentration of some of the elements in his career until then. He then went on to produce a completely new kind of work, the parable for church performance, in 1964.

Also the following year, in the speech accepting the Aspen Award, Britten said: 'I want my music to be of use to people, to please them, to "enhance their lives" (to use Berenson's phrase). I do not write for posterity – in any case, the outlook for that is somewhat uncertain. I write music, now, in Aldeburgh, for people living there, and further afield, indeed for anyone who cares to play it or listen to it.'

It is hard to believe that Britten really has no concern for posterity. In view of the fact that he said it, however, one must accept it at its face value, though possibly if questioned now he would say that he does not write *consciously* for posterity. Certainly the fact that he is now recording several of his works would seem to contradict what he said about posterity, also what he said in the same speech about lamenting the advent of the radio and gramophone, for the following reason:

'One must face the fact today that the vast majority of musical performances take place as far away from the original as it is possible to imagine... Anyone, anywhere, at any time, can listen to the B minor Mass upon one condition only – that they possess a machine. No qualification is required of any sort – faith, virtue, education, experience, age. Music is now free for all... Music demands more from a listener than simply the possession of a tape-machine or a transistor radio... It demands as much effort on the listener's part as the other two corners of the triangle, this holy triangle of composer, performer and listener.'

In providing recordings of his works, Britten is to a certain extent going against his convictions. Of course in this way he is ensuring that there is available a performance of his work as he would like it preserved. But in involving the listener so closely in this triangle for the ideal musical experience, it does not mean that Britten throws the whole responsibility on to the shoulders of the listener. He also has a very precise idea of what the composer's part in this is, and that in turn hinges on the composer's place in society. He had made this quite clear in the speech he delivered when he was made a Freeman of the Borough of Aldeburgh two years previously, in 1962.

'I believe that an artist should be part of his community, should work for it, with it, and be used by it. Over the last hundred years this has become rarer and rarer and the artist and the community have suffered in many cases because without an audience, or with only a highbrow one – without, therefore, a direct contact with his public – his work tends to become "ivory tower", without focus. This has made a great deal of modern work obscure and impractical: only useable by highly skilled performers and only understandable by the most erudite. Don't please think that I am against all new and strange ideas. Far from it; new ideas have a way of seeming odd and surprising when heard for the first time. But I am against experiment for experiment's sake, originality at all costs. It's necessary to say this because there are audiences who are not discriminating about it. They think that everything new is good; that if it is shocking it must be important. There is all the difference in the world... between Stravinsky and electronic experimenters...'

This would seem to bring Britten down fairly and squarely on the side of reaction, and yet there are still people to whom most of his music is as obscure as the electronics he mentioned. They tend to become fewer each year, and even the least adventurous of them eventually manage to find something of his that they can accept. And yet there is another side to this particular coin, which is that a good many of the younger generation of musicians – both composers and performers – find Britten's music positively old fashioned. He is no longer the *avant-garde* composer of thirty, or even twenty, years ago. Indeed, in the eyes of these people, there is an element of the precious in Britten's music which they find hard to accept. And this is by no means the point of view of the more extreme members of the rising generation of musicians. These are not the electronic experimenters, but people who follow in a tradition that leads back directly into the 19th century. They

Peter Pears reliving a moment from *Albert Herring* on the beach at Aldeburgh during recordings of the work. It was in this opera that Britten developed further his flair for word setting

often have as little sympathy with the machines as Britten himself. But do they have the same considerations at the core of their musical being?

One feels instinctively in Britten's music that the machines could never take over. His music will always be for people, and need people to perform it. Hence his attitude to certain contemporary composers. He is not against them so much for the music they write, as for the attitude of mind that is behind the music, though obviously the one very much dictates the other.

Of the present generation Britten has said: 'I find it very worrying that our contemporary young composers are not able to write things for the young or amateurs to play and sing.'

This is not to say that Britten is against all contemporary composers as such, and indeed the Aldeburgh Festival has encouraged many of them. Moreover, Britten knows how beneficial it can be for a composer to be able to hear his works in performance, and it certainly would have helped him if he had been able to hear some of his works performed sooner.

It has almost always been extremely difficult for a young composer to live by his work, and even today many people still do not regard composers as having professional status in their own right. Even when a composer begins to establish himself and make a name for himself, however, there are dangers, for pressure groups, snobs and critics tend – in Britten's estimation – to force him to write not what he has within him, but what they feel he should write. In this respect Britten learnt by bitter experience. In his early days he had to bear some very bitter blows from critics.

What irritated him most was the patronising criticism, and particularly the ill-informed. In an article in *Opera* for March 1952, he recalled how, after a performance of his Three Two-part songs for female voices to words by Walter de la Mare in 1932, one critic accused them of being copies of Walton's three songs from *Façade*. Britten was furious, and at the same time dismayed, because it was quite evident that what the critic said was nonsense, but even more so, for a young composer, it was terribly discouraging. On another occasion a critic praised the fact that the work being performed was brief, and 'closed down in good time'.

At the time of his fiftieth birthday Britten said that in view of all the works behind him, people seemed to think that he must be bursting with confidence for the future, but he said that this was not the case. He had not then achieved the simplicity that he was after in his music, and he felt that he was still far from the standard of technical achievement that Bridge had educated him to. In fact the 'cello *Symphony* of 1963, the year of his fiftieth birthday, seemed to herald a new kind of asceticism in Britten's music, a spareness that he seemed to be looking for. *Curlew River* (1964) was another step along this road. Even so, Britten has never ceased to be able to write music that is 'grateful' for performers, and *The Golden Vanity* (1966) is a good example of this.

Britten with the score of *Gloriana*. Since its première at Covent Garden the opera had been somewhat neglected until a concert performance was mounted on Britten's fiftieth birthday in 1963. Sylvia Fisher sang the role of the queen then, and it was she who took the part in the revival three years later at Sadler's Wells

As to confidence, however, this is questionable. Some people detect a distinct lack of confidence in him at present, a lack of sense of direction. Others would go even further than this, and say that the real Britten was lost as long ago as somewhere on the trip to America, and that all that has happened since then has been merely a waste of talent or a failure to realise initial promise. This view makes one wonder how on earth one explains away some of the amazing successes that Britten has had in the meantime, though of course success is by no means always synonymous with quality, especially in the arts.

He has been criticised by one habitually perceptive musician for being puritanical, and of being unwilling to let his music go to climax. It is certainly easier to think of moments of anguish in Britten's music than it is to think of the moments of intense joy. There has, however, always been deep solace in Britten's music. Anyone who could write such a calming cadence as on the word 'comforter' in the *Te Deum* in C, or convey such a

99

Previous page: Britten conducting a performance of Bach's St John Passion, one of his favourite works, at the Proms in the Albert Hall, London, in July 1967 – almost thirty years after his first appearance there in the Queen's Hall days

Britten in the garden of his home, the Red House, at Aldeburgh. He has always been fond of the work of the Austrian sculptor Georg Ehrlich, who executed a bronze head of Britten in addition to his other work at Aldeburgh

profound sense of stillness and calm as in the chorus that ends the first act of *A Midsummer Night's Dream*, must be a very humane person, and it was for his humanity that he was given the Aspen Award.

Britten has never forgotten human beings, ordinary people. As the Cambridge University Orator said in 1959 of Britten: 'Although his works are of a most subtle originality, and are indeed approved by the *avant-garde*, yet they are not lost on the less instructed. And there is no one for whom he makes music more readily than for boys and girls. These he delights to conduct himself, these he entices to make an opera with him, to these he introduces the several instruments of the orchestra, and with many of them he carries on a regular correspondence.'

It is perhaps bitterly ironical, then, that some of the children that Britten may have helped along the road towards a musical career are now the very ones who find his music so dated, and in some cases no longer capable of saying anything to them. Educational techniques have changed so radically over the last twenty or twenty-five years that it is very easy to fail to appreciate the immense amount that the entire approach to the teaching of music owes to Britten. In addition to purely technical achievement, he has helped create a general ambiance for introducing children to music which has totally transformed what went before.

This is to a certain extent one of the eternal dilemmas, that of the pupil who outgrows his teacher, and Britten must remember the frustrating time that he experienced at the Royal College. Not only was his talent not catered for there, but even when he tried to help himself he was thwarted.

Britten's work with and for children will surely be one of the most lasting elements in the whole of his life and work. Few composers, anywhere in the world, can have done more than he has – virtually single handed – to improve the standard of musical education of children. One trusts that he will never stop writing for them, and that they never cease to occupy the place that they have occupied hitherto in his musical conscience. He said in 1960: 'As I get older, I find that I increasingly prefer the work either of the very young or of the very old.' In point of fact he said this in reference to Shakespeare's play *A Midsummer Night's Dream*, which he feels is a play by a young man, irrespective of how old Shakespeare actually was when he wrote it. One feels that the Hölderlin fragments that Britten set are, on the other hand, definitely the work of an old man.

To speculate on what Britten may or may not produce in the future is foolishness, especially in view of the way that his career has at times suddenly moved in an apparently totally new direction. There are, however, one or two other directions that he might explore further. Perhaps some more chamber music. The *Sonata* for 'cello and piano has been a welcome addition, as well as the *Gemini Variations*, but since the *String Quartet* No. 2 there has been precious little that would involve a small group of people making chamber music. Of course, as with the string quartet, Britten may feel that the classic form of piano quartet or quintet is not one that he can speak through, particularly at this stage in his career, and of course opera, and vocal music generally, occupies a large part of his attention.

This suggests another direction which one might hope for development. One of the works that Britten withdrew was Opus 17, a series of settings for unaccompanied chorus of words by Gerard Manley Hopkins, the Jesuit poet, dating from 1939. Opus 16 had also been withdrawn. It is a pity that Britten has not so far returned to Hopkins – a poet who has written some of the most exciting verse in the English language. It is admittedly some of the most difficult both in meaning and rhythm.

Britten and Hopkins should make a good combination, especially since they both have such a high regard for Purcell. In a letter of 1878, Hopkins wrote: 'I quite agree with what you write about Milton. His verse as one reads it seems something necessary and eternal (so to me does Purcell's music).' In Hopkins, living when he did, this was a rare enough thing. He even wrote a poem entitled *Henry Purcell*, and gave it the following preface. 'The poet wishes well to the divine genius of Purcell and praises him that, whereas other musicians have given utterance to the moods of man's mind, he has, beyond that, uttered in notes the very make and species of man as created both in him and in all men generally.' This sounds remarkably like U Thant's citation when Britten's United Nations anthem was first performed, and articulates what the people who most like Britten's music generally feel about his genius.

Hopkins was something of a composer himself, and sent his settings to a professional composer, Sir Robert Stewart, for criticism. He was therefore alive to the finer points of Purcell's music, and at the same time aware of the problems confronting composers when they come to set words to music. But over and above the specifically musical considerations, Hopkins set great store by what he called 'inscape' – the revelation of the inner nature of things, which leads ultimately to one's perception of God in the world. Indeed, it was for this very quality that Hopkins appreciated Purcell's music, as one sees from the quotation above.

Britten has great depth of insight into certain people, and into certain composers and their music. He seems to have an acute perception of the possibilities of things, whether it be words, musical instruments, possible combinations, or a dramatic situation, which is close to perceiving the inscape so beloved of Hopkins.

Britten's perception does not lead him automatically to the Christian God, as did Hopkins', and in fact his religious convictions are not made explicit in his music, despite much overt reference to and involvement with specifically Christian sentiments. It is really human response that most matters to Britten. People tend to be redeemed or damned by other people in his operas – not by their response or lack of response to God.

Britten's perception, or inherent flair, dates from a very early age, though he himself said that Bridge taught him to think and feel through the instruments he was writing for, in other words he does not simply write *for* an instrument, but *through* it, which is a vastly different thing, and explains – in part, at least – why he writes so successfully for instruments and voices too. When Britten intended beginning *On This Island* with a downward *glissando* on the piano, Bridge said that he was trying to make something non-tonal out of the piano, such as a side drum, so instead Britten made it a downward D major arpeggio. In a sense Britten was anticipating by a number of years what many contemporary composers have been doing for the last ten or fifteen. Instruments are no longer used in a way that their unique characteristics are exploited. The piano in particular has come in for a great deal of misuse, largely because it is the instrument most readily available. In contemporary music it is struck with hammers, its strings are rasped or plucked and its keyboard has even been sat on. It seems an extraordinary waste of decades of work in perfecting so subtle an instrument as a modern grand piano, and would seem to have gloomy implications for the future of musical instruments if this sort of treatment is to become widespread.

In writing for instruments Britten has always upheld the characteristics of the instruments themselves, and often he has enriched the literature and extended their range. He does not

Benjamin Britten outside Blythburgh Parish Church in 1969, the year of the Maltings fire. The festival programme had to be rearranged overnight, and the planned performances of Mozart's *Idomeneo* had to take place in this church

impose music on the instrument, but writes in a way that his music speaks through the instrument. In a similar way his dramatic sense speaks through the situation on stage. It was this combination of insight and flair for isolating the essential characteristics that made *Curlew River* such a success.

And yet one would not describe Britten as a mystic, certainly not when one thinks of a composer such as Michael Tippett, with whom Britten has been friendly for many years. Tippett contributed to Britten's fiftieth birthday by dedicating his *Concerto for Orchestra*, commissioned by the Edinburgh Festival, to him 'with affection and admiration in the year of his fiftieth birthday'. Britten, one feels, is much more rigorously practical than Tippett. It is still too early to tell, but on the evidence of what he has written so far, it would seem unlikely that Britten would ever write such an opera as Tippett's *The Knot Garden*. Conversely, from what one knows of Tippett's work, it is unlikely that he would now have written the *War Requiem*, which even some of Britten's most fervent admirers confess to having found — albeit in retrospect — somewhat trite in parts.

This should not, however, allow us to forget Britten's apparently inexhaustible store of flashes of genius. In *Canticle Two* (Abraham and Isaac), for example, only two voices are involved. The tenor sings Abraham and the alto the boy Isaac. For the third voice, the voice of God, Britten had the brilliant idea of having both voices singing together. In this way he created one voice out of two. This brilliance was manifest from an early age. As Tippett has said: 'Music seems to flow out of his mind, out of his body ... I am endlessly curious for what may come next.' With the passage of time it is all too easy to forget how precocious Britten was as a child — almost as precocious as the young Mozart. He was five when he began composing, and began to have harmony lessons when he was ten. When he was twelve he wrote an overture in B flat minor for full orchestra. There are ninety-one pages of the full score, written during the end-of-term school exams and sports and cricket matches.

There was an amazing intrepidity from the very beginning, but has he, as some people maintain, always 'played safe', and avoided risks in his music? There are those who would say that he undoubtedly has. But there again, examples spring to mind where, from a practical point of view, Britten has taken something of a gamble.

In casting *A Midsummer Night's Dream*, for example, the way he did, he limited himself considerably, and thereby took a large risk. In particular, the role of Oberon being written for a counter-tenor, and a particular counter-tenor — Alfred Deller — at that. The range is very restricted, and the subsequent generation of counter-tenors, whilst fully acknowledging the way in which Deller virtually pioneered the way in this century for the acceptance of the counter-tenor voice on the concert platform once more, are now more versatile vocally. Many of them feel more at home in a higher register, for instance. Much of Britten's music for Oberon revolves around the E flat above middle C, which is only really the beginning of the most effective part of the modern counter-tenor's register. This is one of the few examples where Britten's involvement with one particular voice may have been a restricting, rather than broadening influence. By way of contrast, the part of Isaac in *Canticle Two*, conceived for a contralto, and with a much higher overall tessitura than the music for Oberon, is now often sung by a counter-tenor.

Apart from the rather specialised consideration about the role of Oberon — but one which is nevertheless crucial to the opera, since Oberon is one of the leading characters — there is also the question of the use of boys' voices for the fairies. This may present a problem in countries where there is no tradition of choirs, or certainly boys' choirs, to draw on, and female voices do not give the same effect at all. Their tone tends to be much less clearly focused than that of boys, and therefore lacks the incisive quality that Britten looks for. Musically, of course, *A Midsummer Night's Dream* is a delightful opera, and one sincerely hopes that it will be kept alive. As long as the Aldeburgh Festival and the English Opera Group last this can be assured, but one hopes that Covent Garden and other opera houses will keep it in their repertoire, too.

It is probably for his operas that Britten is chiefly known around the world. In his own country Britten was made a Companion of Honour in 1952, and awarded the Order of Merit in 1965. By the time this book is published he will have received many tributes in honour of his sixtieth birthday. He has numerous honorary doctorates, and one suspects that some day he may be offered the post of Master of the Queen's Musick. This, in the eyes of some, would be a sign of his total identification with the Establishment. It would be in the composer's own works, however, that the truth would be revealed.

Catalogue of Works

The works listed here are those which have been published; for a list of those performed but unpublished, up to and including 1960, the reader is referred to the catalogue published on the composer's fiftieth birthday in 1963. This also contains details of arrangements and Purcell realisations

1929

The Birds
Song for medium voice and piano, words by Hilaire Belloc (revised 1934)

A Wealden Trio
Song of the Women, words by Ford Madox Ford (edited by composer 1968)

1930

Tit for Tat
Five boyhood settings composed between 1927 and 1930, words by Walter de la Mare (edited by composer 1969)

A Hymn to the Virgin
Unaccompanied anthem for mixed voices, words anonymous (revised 1934)

The Sycamore Tree
Unaccompanied mixed chorus, words traditional (edited by composer 1968)

1931

Sweet was the Song
Contralto and female chorus, from an unpublished Christmas suite entitled *Thy King's Birthday* (edited by composer 1968)

1932

Three two-part songs
Boys' or women's voices and piano, words by Walter de la Mare. The third song, *The Ship of Rio*, was arranged by the composer for solo voice and piano and published in 1963

Sinfonietta, Opus 1
Chamber orchestra

Phantasy, Opus 2
Quartet in one movement for oboe, violin, viola and 'cello

1933

A Boy was Born, Opus 3
Choral variations for unaccompanied mixed voices, words from

Ancient English Carols and the Oxford Book of Carols (revised 1955). Variation 5, *Corpus Christi Carol*, was arranged by the composer in 1961 for treble solo, or unison voices, and organ

Two Part Songs
Mixed voices and piano, words by George Wither and Robert Graves

1934

Simple Symphony, Opus 4
String orchestra or string quartet

Holiday Diary, Opus 5
Suite for piano

Friday Afternoons, Opus 7
Twelve songs for children's voices and piano, in two volumes, words from various sources

May
Unison song and piano, words anonymous

1935

Suite, Opus 6
Violin and piano

Te Deum in C Major
Treble solo, mixed voices and organ. A *Jubilate* in C Major was published in 1961

1936

Our Hunting Fathers, Opus 8
Symphonic cycle for high voice and orchestra, text devised by W. H. Auden

Soirées Musicales, Opus 9
Suite of five movements from Rossini for orchestra

1937

Pacifist March
Unison song with accompaniment, words by Ronald Duncan

Variations on a Theme of Frank Bridge, Opus 10
String orchestra

On this Island, Opus 11
Five songs for high voice and piano, words by W. H. Auden

Two Ballads
Two voices and piano, words by Montagu Slater and W. H. Auden

Fish in the Unruffled Lakes
Song for high voice and piano, words by W. H. Auden

Mont Juic, Opus 12 (with Lennox Berkeley)
Suite of Catalan dances for orchestra

1938

Piano Concerto No. 1 in D, Opus 13
Revised 1945

Advance Democracy
Unaccompanied double mixed chorus, words by Randall Swingler

1939

Ballad of Heroes, Opus 14
Tenor or soprano solo, chorus and orchestra, words by W. H. Auden and Randall Swingler

Violin Concerto, Opus 15
Revised 1958

Young Apollo, Opus 16
Piano and string orchestra, withdrawn

Poems of Gerard Manley Hopkins, Opus 17
Unaccompanied mixed chorus, withdrawn

Les Illuminations, Opus 18
High voice and string orchestra, words by Arthur Rimbaud

Canadian Carnival – Kermesse Canadienne, Opus 19
Orchestra

1940

Sinfonia da Requiem, Opus 20
Orchestra

Diversions on a Theme, Opus 21
Piano (left hand) and orchestra, revised 1954

Seven Sonnets of Michelangelo, Opus 22
Tenor and piano

Introduction and Rondo alla Burlesca, Opus 23, No. 1
Two pianos

1941

Paul Bunyan
Operetta, libretto by W. H. Auden, withdrawn

Mazurka Elegiaca, Opus 23, No. 2
Two pianos

Matinées Musicales, Opus 24
Second suite of five movements from Rossini for orchestra

String Quartet No. 1 in D, Opus 25

Scottish Ballad, Opus 26
Two pianos and orchestra

1942

Hymn to St Cecilia, Opus 27
Unaccompanied mixed voices, words by W. H. Auden

A Ceremony of Carols, Opus 28
Treble voices and harp, words by William Cornish, Robert Southwell, James, John and Robert Wedderburn and from anonymous sources

1943

Prelude and Fugue, Opus 29
Eighteen-part string orchestra

Rejoice in the Lamb, Opus 30
Festival cantata for treble, alto, tenor and bass solo, mixed chorus and organ, words by Christopher Smart

Serenade, Opus 31
Tenor, horn and strings, words by Cotton, Tennyson, Blake, Jonson, Keats and an anonymous source

The Ballad of Little Musgrave and Lady Barnard
Male voices and piano, words anonymous

1944

A Shepherd's Carol
Unaccompanied mixed voices, words by W. H. Auden

Chorale, after an old French Carol
Unaccompanied double mixed chorus, words by W. H. Auden

1945

Peter Grimes, Opus 33
Opera, libretto by Montagu Slater from a poem of George Crabbe

Festival Te Deum, Opus 32
Mixed chorus and organ

The Holy Sonnets of John Donne, Opus 35
High voice and piano

String Quartet No. 2 in C, Opus 36

1946

The Young Person's Guide to the Orchestra, Opus 34
Variations and fugue on a theme of Purcell for orchestra

The Rape of Lucretia, Opus 37
Opera, libretto by Ronald Duncan after the play by André Obey, revised 1947

Prelude and Fugue on a Theme of Vittoria
Organ

Occasional Overture in C, Opus 38
Orchestra, withdrawn

1947

Albert Herring, Opus 39
Opera, libretto by Eric Crozier from a short story by Guy de Maupassant

Canticle 1, Opus 40
High voice and piano, words by Francis Quarles

A Charm of Lullabies, Opus 41
Mezzo soprano and piano, words by Blake, Burns, Robert Greene, Thomas Randolph and John Philip

1948

Saint Nicolas, Opus 42
Cantata for tenor solo, mixed chorus, string orchestra, piano duet, percussion and organ, words by Eric Crozier

The Beggar's Opera, Opus 43
Realisation of the ballad opera by John Gay (1728)

1949

Spring Symphony, Opus 44
Soprano, alto and tenor solo, mixed chorus boys' choir and orchestra, words from several sources

The Little Sweep, Opus 45
Opera for young people, libretto by Eric Crozier

A Wedding Anthem – Amo Ergo Sum, Opus 46
Soprano and tenor solo, mixed chorus and organ, words by Ronald Duncan

1950

Five Flower Songs, Opus 47
Unaccompanied mixed chorus, words by Herrick, Crabbe, Clare and from an anonymous source

Lachrymae, Opus 48
Reflections on a song of John Dowland for viola and piano

1951

Six Metamorphoses after Ovid, Opus 49
Oboe solo

Billy Budd, Opus 50
Opera, libretto by E. M. Forster and Eric Crozier from the story by Herman Melville, revised 1960

1952

Canticle II – Abraham and Isaac, Opus 51
Alto, tenor and piano, words from the Chester miracle play

1953

Gloriana, Opus 53
Opera, libretto by William Plomer

Winter Words, Opus 52
High voice and piano, lyrics and ballads by Thomas Hardy

1954

The Turn of the Screw, Opus 54
Opera, libretto by Myfanwy Piper after the story by Henry James

Canticle III – Still Falls the Rain, Opus 55
Tenor, horn and piano, words by Edith Sitwell

1955

Alpine Suite
Recorder trio

Scherzo
Recorder quartet

Hymn to Saint Peter, Opus 56a
Treble solo, mixed chorus and organ, words from the Gradual of the Feast of St Peter and St Paul

Antiphon, Opus 56b
Mixed chorus and organ, words by George Herbert

The Prince of the Pagodas, Opus 57
Ballet

1957

Songs from the Chinese, Opus 58
High voice and guitar, words by Chinese poets translated by Arthur Waley

Noye's Fludde, Opus 59
Chester miracle play set for mixed voices, children's chorus, chamber ensemble and children's orchestra

1958

Nocturne, Opus 60
Tenor, seven obbligato instruments and string orchestra, words by Shelley, Tennyson, Coleridge, Middleton, Wordsworth, Owen, Keats and Shakespeare

Six Hölderlin Fragments, Opus 61
Voice and piano

1959

Cantata Academica – Carmen Basiliense, Opus 62
Soprano, alto, tenor and bass solo, mixed chorus and orchestra, words from the university charter and older orations in praise of the city

Fanfare for Three Trumpets
Written for the Magna Carta pageant at St Edmundsbury

Missa Brevis in D, Opus 63
Boys' voices and organ

1960

A Midsummer Night's Dream, Opus 64
Opera, libretto adapted from Shakespeare by Benjamin Britten and Peter Pears

1961

Sonata in C, Opus 65
'Cello and piano

Jubilate Deo in C
Mixed choir and organ

War Requiem, Opus 66
Soprano, tenor and baritone solo, mixed chorus, orchestra, chamber orchestra, boys' choir and organ, words from the *Missa pro Defunctis* and Wilfred Owen

1962

Psalm 150, Opus 67
Two-part children's voices and instruments

A Hymn of Saint Columba – Regis regum rectissimi
Mixed chorus and organ

1963

Symphony for 'Cello and Orchestra, Opus 68

Night Piece – Notturno
Piano

Cantata Misericordium, Opus 69
Tenor and baritone solo, small chorus and string orchestra, piano, harp and timpani, Latin words by Patrick Wilkinson

1964

Cadenzas for Haydn's 'Cello Concerto in C

Nocturnal – after John Dowland, Opus 70
Guitar

Curlew River, Opus 71
Parable for church performance, text by William Plomer after the Japanese Noh play *Sumidagawa*

1965

Suite No. 1 in G Major, Opus 72
'Cello

Gemini Variations, Opus 73
Flute, violin and piano (four hands)

Songs and Proverbs of William Blake, Opus 74
Baritone and piano

Voices for Today, Opus 75
Anthem for mixed chorus and boys' chorus, organ optional, words from various sources

The Poet's Echo, Opus 76
High voice and piano, words by Pushkin

1966

The Burning Fiery Furnace, Opus 77
Second parable for church performance, words by William Plomer

The Golden Vanity, Opus 78
Vaudeville for boys' voices and piano, words by Colin Graham after an old English ballad

Cadenzas for Mozart's Piano Concerto in E flat Major (K. 482)

1967

Overture – The Building of the House, Opus 79
Chorus and orchestra

Suite No. 2 in D Major, Opus 80
'Cello

1968

The Prodigal Son, Opus 81
Third parable for church performance, words by William Plomer

1969

Children's Crusade, Opus 82
Ballad for boys' choir and orchestra, words by Bertold Brecht

Suite in C, Opus 83
Harp

Who are these Children? Opus 84
High voice and piano, lyrics, rhymes and riddles by William Soutar

1970

Owen Wingrave, Opus 85
Opera, libretto by Myfanwy Piper from the story by Henry James

1971

Canticle IV – The Journey of the Magi, Opus 86
Counter-tenor, tenor, bass and piano, words by T. S. Eliot

Suite No. 3, Opus 87
'Cello (based on Russian themes)

1972

Death in Venice, Opus 88
Opera, libretto by Myfanwy Piper from the novel by Thomas Mann

Index

Numerals in italics refer to illustrations

Aldeburgh *19*, *25*, 33, 34, 71
Aldeburgh Festival 45–9, 51–4
Alston, Audrey 9, 73
Ansermet, Ernest 26
Astle, Ethel 9
Auden, W. H. 9, 12, 13, *14*, 15, 16, 20, 25

Barbirolli, John 19, 74
Bartlett, Ethel 73
Benjamin, Arthur 11, 71
Berg, Alban 12, *12*
Bergmann, Walter 23
Berkeley, Lennox 46
Brain, Dennis 23, 48, 73
Bream, Julian 48
Bridge, Frank 9, *10*, 11, 23, 46, 71, 73, 88, 103; *The Sea* 9, *10*
British Broadcasting Corporation 15–16, 40
Britten, Benjamin childhood 9; viola playing 9, 73; schooling 9–11; on Frank Bridge 11; G.P.O. Film Unit 12–15; and commissions 13; in America 15–20; and pacificism 15; children's voices 49–52; as pianist 62, 71; and folksong 62–7, 94; and church music 51, 64–6; method of composing 71; orchestration 74–9
   Works: (*see also* page 106)
      Albert Herring (Op. 39) 26, *27*, 28
      Ballad of Heroes (Op. 14) 16
      Beggar's Opera (Op. 43) 28, 94
      Billy Budd (Op. 50) 26, 29–30, *36–7*
      Burning Fiery Furnace (Op. 77) 40, *40*
      Canadian Carnival – Kermesse canadienne (Op. 19) 16
      Canticle II – Abraham and Isaac (Op. 51) 104
      Ceremony of Carols (Op. 28) 40, 50, 61, 65–6
      Curlew River (Op. 71) 34–9, 82
      Death in Venice (Op. 88) 41, *42*
      Gemini Variations (Op. 73) 52
      Gloriana (Op. 53) 30–2
      Holy Sonnets of John Donne (Op. 35) 13, 23–4
      Hymn to St Cecilia (Op. 27) 9, 15, 65
      Hymn to the Virgin 64
      Les Illuminations (Op. 18) 13, 16, 60
      Let's Make an Opera (The Little Sweep) (Op. 45) 28–9, *29*
      Midsummer Night's Dream (Op. 64) 34, 81–2, 89, *93*, 104
      Missa Brevis (Op. 63) 51
      Nocturne (Op. 60) 73
      Noye's Fludde (Op. 59) 33–4, 74
      Occasional Overture (Op. 38 – withdrawn) 16
      On this Island (Op. 11) 15
      Our Hunting Fathers (Op. 8) 13, 15
      Owen Wingrave (Op. 85) 40–1, *42–3*, 78
      Paul Bunyan 15, 25–6
      Peter Grimes (Op. 33) 20, *23*, 24, 25, *25*, 26, 92
      Poet's Echo (Op. 76) 49, 69
      Prelude and Fugue (Op. 29) 74
      Prince of the Pagodas (Op. 57) 33, 79–81, *80–1*
      Prodigal Son (Op. 81) *10*, 40
      Rape of Lucretia (Op. 37) 16, 26, 28
      Rejoice in the Lamb (Op. 30) 45, 66
      St Nicolas (Op. 42) 28, 33, 45, 66
      Serenade (Op. 31) 23, 50
      Seven Sonnets of Michelangelo (Op. 22) 16, 23
      Simple Symphony (Op. 4) 74
      Sinfonia da Requiem (Op. 20) 16–19, 20
      Sinfonietta (Op. 1) 11, 12
      String Quartet No. 1 (Op. 25) 16
      Turn of the Screw (Op. 54) 32–3
      Variations on a Theme of Frank Bridge (Op. 10) 11, 16, 73
      Violin Concerto (Op. 15) 16
      War Requiem (Op. 66) 86–8
      Young Person's Guide to the Orchestra (Op. 34) 15

Brosa, Antonio 74

Cambridge University 13, 46
Cocteau, Jean 16
Coleman, Basil 30, *32*, 33
Copland, Aaron 20, 72
Crabbe, George 20
Cross, Joan 25, *31*, 32
Crozier, Eric *19*, 25, *25*, 26, 28, 29

Duncan, Ronald 16, 26, *27*

Elgar, Edward 94
Ellis, Osian 51
Eyck, Jan van (*St Cecilia*) 2

Fischer-Dieskau, Dietrich 48
Ferrier, Kathleen 48
Forster, E. M. 20, *21*, 29, 45

G.P.O. Film Unit (*Coal Face* and *Night Mail*) 12–15, 79
Glyndebourne 26
Goodall, Reginald 25, 26, *27*
Goossens, Eugene *19*, 73
Gresham's School, Holt (Norfolk) 11
Grierson, John 12
Guthrie, Tyrone *59*

Hawkes, Ralph 12–13
Holst, Imogen *65*, 71, 91, 92
Hopkins, Gerard Manley 15, 103

Ireland, John 11–12
Isherwood, Christopher 13, *14*, 15, 16, 24

Kodály, Zoltán *48*, 52
Koussevitzky, Serge 20, *21*

Lambert, Constant 64
Leigh, Walter 15
Lowestoft 9, *9*

MacNeice, Louis 13, *13*, 15, 20
Mahler, Gustav 41, 46, *90*, 94
Malvern 12
Menuhin, Yehudi 23, *24*
Mercury Theatre (Macnaghten–Lemare Concerts) 12, 24, 64
Moore, Henry 66, *67*
Musique concrète 15

New York 16, 19
Nolan, Sydney 45, *67*
Norwich 9

Owen, Wilfred *39*, 86

Paderewski 73
Pears, Peter 16, *19*, 20, 23, 24, 25, *25*, *27*, *31*, *32*, 33, *40*, 41, 45, 46, 54, *63*, 69, 73, *73*, 94, 98
Piper, John *19*, 26, 28, 30, *32*, 33, 52
Piper, Myfanwy 32, *32*, 41, 52, 60
Plomer, William 33, 40
Priestley, J. B. 16
Purcell, Henry 15, 23, 46, 52, 79, 88–94, *90*, 103; *Dido and Aeneas* 26, 28, 91

Rembrandt (*The Return of the Prodigal Son*) *38*, 40
Richter, Sviatoslav 49, 73
Robertson, Rae 73
Rossini 15, 79
Rostropovich, Msitslav 48–9, *48*, 62, *68*, 69
Royal College of Music, London 11–12

Sackville-West, Edward 15
Samuel, Harold 11

Schoenberg 79;
   Pierrot Lunaire 12
Shostakovich, Dmitri 49
Sitwell, Edith *90*, 91
Slater, Montagu 24
Snape 20, 72;
   The Maltings 45–6, *45*, *47*, 54, *56–7*
Stravinsky 11, 79
Sutherland, Graham 66, *67*
Swingler, Randall 16

Tippett, Michael 23, *23*, 46, 91–2, 104

U Thant 81, 103

Venice *32*, *35*, 40, 71;
   Fenice Theatre 33, *35*
Vienna 12
Vishnevskaya, Galina 49, *59*, *68*, 69

White, T. H. 15
Wilkinson, Patrick 60
Wittgenstein, Paul 72
Wright, Basil 12

The publishers are grateful to the following people who very kindly supplied illustrations:

Colour
Erich Auerbach: 17, 96; BBC: 78t, b; Decca Record Company: 18, 55, 56, 58, 75; G. A. Johnson (Ove Aarup & Associates): 57; Mansell Collection: 35; John Massey Stuart: 38; Houston Rogers: 95; Edwin Smith: 76–77; Roger Wood: 36–37

Black & White
Erich Auerbach: 32, 88, 89, 93; BBC: 25L; Boosey & Hawkes: 19t, b; by kind permission of the Revd. Bulstrode: 30, 86t; by kind permission of St Matthew's, Northampton: 67t, m; Camera Press: 49r, 83t; Central Press: 105; Conway Picture Library: 32, 48r, 70, 84, 99; Milein Cosman: 50; Decca Record Company: 22, 40, 41, 52, 53, 63, 98, 102; Daily Mirror (Ove Aarup & Associates): 44; John Donat (Ove Aarup & Associates): 47; East Anglian Newspapers Ltd: 87; Faber Music Ltd: 11; Hamlyn Publishing Group: 12t; Ford Jenkins: frontispiece, 8, 29; Keystone: 27tr, 51, 82L; Lowestoft Journal: 9t; G. Macdomnic: 100–101; Mansell Collection: 9b, 90t; Sidney Nolan: 67b; Norwich Central Library: 10; Novosti: 49L, 59b, 68, 69; Oxford University Press: 39; P & O Ltd: 86b; Popperfoto: 21, 57t, 82r; Radio Times Hulton Picture Library: 13, 14, 20, 23, 25r, 27tL, 59t, 60, 65, 72, 90L; The Rambert School of Ballet: 12b; Houston Rogers: 80, 81; Brian Seed: 48L; Edwin Smith: 61; Reg Wilson: 43; Roger Wood: 27b, 31, 45–46, 83b; UPI: 24; Anthony Crickmay: 42.

Bibliography

Benjamin Britten. A Commentary on his Works from a Group of Specialists, edited by Donald Mitchell and Hans Keller. London, 1952

Benjamin Britten: a complete catalogue of his works. London, 1963

British Composers in Interview, Murray Schafer. London, 1963

Tribute to Benjamin Britten on his Fiftieth Birthday, edited by Anthony Gishford. London, 1963

On Receiving the First Aspen Award, Benjamin Britten. London, 1964

Benjamin Britten, Michael Hurd. London, 1966

Benjamin Britten, Percy M. Young. London, 1966

The Operas of Benjamin Britten, Patricia Howard. London, 1969

Benjamin Britten: his life and operas, Eric Walter White. Revised edition, London, 1970

Britten, Imogen Holst. Second edition, London, 1970